Lucid

Dreaming

The Ultimate Guide on How to Literally Live Your Dreams

(How to Become Conscious While Sleeping and Control the Storyline of Your Dreams)

Tony Christie

Published By **Zoe Lawson**

Tony Christie

Lucid Dreaming: The Ultimate Guide on How to Literally Live Your Dreams (How to Become Conscious While Sleeping and Control the Storyline of Your Dreams)

ISBN 978-1-998927-10-4

No part of this guidebook shall be reproduced in any form without permission in writing from the publisher except in the case of brief quotations embodied in critical articles or reviews.

Legal & Disclaimer

The information contained in this book is not designed to replace or take the place of any form of medicine or professional medical advice. The information in this book has been provided for educational & entertainment purposes only.

The information contained in this book has been compiled from sources deemed reliable, and it is accurate to the best of the Author's knowledge; however, the Author cannot guarantee its accuracy and validity and cannot be held liable for any errors or omissions. Changes are periodically made to this book. You must consult your doctor or get professional medical advice before using any of the suggested remedies, techniques, or information in this book.

Table Of Contents

Chapter 1: Why The Lucid Dream?

More importantly, why are we able to do it? Although it is able to appear banal, this query is essential if we want to get the maximum out of lucid dreaming. If we ask ourselves why regularly sufficient, we will in the long run locate the idea preference that turn out to be hidden till now.

This is exactly why we need to ask this vital and reputedly simple question. It allows us to find out what lies below our popularity. It is the start of lucid dreaming, a exercise that allows us to enter the unconscious and aware geographical regions to get better factors of ourselves.

Concentration is the vital detail to lucid dreaming. To reap lucidity in an altered nation, maximum of the capabilities essential for it require you to be privy to your sensations and use them to come to be aware about the states of reputation you're in. You can then manipulate how you have interaction in the ones states. All of this requires a easy and targeted technique. This form of reputation starts with articulating why you are doing this.

Whether you are new to lucid dreaming or an professional practitioner, take a moment to ask your self: Why are you lucid? Your dreams are masses less likely to carry you the rewards and outcomes you preference. Your course will be extra focused if you understand your motivations for embarking in this journey. Another key to fulfillment is to have a clean vision of your adventure.

There are many superficial solutions that may be placed while you ask why. It is essential to delve deeper into them. Do you aspire to have particular abilities? Do you desire extra pleasure in life? Perhaps it is outstanding to search for motivation in improving yourself-image. Before you recognition your interest on the what, spend a whole lot of time statistics the why. It takes power and time to discover your proper desires and align them with the desires that will help you acquire them.

It is likewise a dynamic question. Over time, the solution may also moreover moreover alternate. The motivations, goals and motives that pressure us nowadays may lose their stress the next day, a year or a decade from now. Our why will change as we develop and analyze, simply as our priorities, beliefs and lives trade.

My first exploration of lucid dreaming turned into for amusement. When I became in my twenties, I would possibly have responded "For fun and to break out from everyday lifestyles" at the same time as asked why I lucid dreamed. But as I discovered out extra approximately the arena of lucid dreaming, I realized there has been loads greater to it than I perception. I positioned that lucid dreaming allowed me to connect to a deeper a part of my Self, in addition to understand its dream worldwide. I started out dreaming of escaping, however ended up dreaming of staying with myself and becoming greater entire.

WHAT TO EXPECT FROM A LUCID DREAM

Acid goals can provoke a massive sort of bodily sensations. All of these sensations are normal and common. The most not unusual sensation is vibrations. They can variety from a moderate tingling to the feeling of the frame dissolving or falling apart. These sensations can be alarming, but they're now not some thing to worry approximately. They recommend that you are getting aware of the approach of falling asleep. Once you loosen up, they may disappear. Take a test the dream revel in I had:

As I nod off, I experience the vibrations that normally get up after I understand I am going to have an out-of-frame dream-like enjoy. I awaken and find out myself in my room. Everything appears slower and I suspect I am dreaming. When I search around my room, I expect I is probably sleepwalking. Everything is sluggish and even though actual. I'm afraid my roommates might be aware I'm taking walks spherical my residence, however I determine it's miles really worth the threat and head to the relaxation room to look in the reflect. . . . .

Although I actually have had many lucid goals earlier than this, this situation suggests how real the lucid dream enjoy may be. It is important to be open to the surprising and to be aware about what you revel in in lucid goals. These standards are especially applicable to your physical sensations and your environment. You can evaluate the dreaming and waking variations of each.

UNDERSTAND YOUR BODY

Lucid dream stories may be scary and complicated. They can also motive lucid dreams to turn out to be poor or give up if they will be no longer understood. You can alter the outcome and path of the dream thru fun your frame.

Certain sensations may be used to provoke lucid desires or particular out-of-frame reviews. A lucid dream or out-of-body experience may be because of way of buzzing sounds. These sounds may be heard at some point of sleep paralysis or in advance than. This kind of dream is regularly associated with paralysis, hypnotic hallucinations, and the sensation of floating or falling. These forms of desires will no longer be as alarming in case you undergo in thoughts that they're not unusual.

REALISM

A man or woman generally checks the surroundings at the same time as he or she starts offevolved to discover a dream. Normal lucid goals incorporate a decrease degree of realism than truth. The dream may additionally moreover moreover incorporate unrealistic characters or unbelievable physics.

In cases wherein human beings have lucid desires with out-of-frame opinions, realism will growth to some unique degree. Out-of-body reviews can result in a heightened attention that the man or woman is dreaming or traveling to some other length of reality. Out-of-body goals frequently have more element than regular lucid dreams. Many dreamers don't forget that out-of-frame reviews are actual three-D studies.

Experiments on out-of-frame stories display that they exceed present day truth checks, indicating that they may be extra than simply lucid goals. The following dream became tested by me, and I supplied it at the start of this financial disaster.

I turn my toilet mild on and off and it virtually works flawlessly. This leads me to consider that I am sleepwalking. I phrase that the whole lot is barely green after I appearance within the replicate. I see my footwear as I stroll down the stairs leading outside. I place my shoes so I can awaken the subsequent morning and notice that I am sleepwalking. I move outdoor and look at the high-quality stars and supernovas. I wander around for some time and then lose lucidity. Then, I actually have an extended sleep. I wake up and understand that my footwear are not placed unusually. I moreover realize that it is about fifteen ranges out of doors. This have to have made me wake up if my drowsing garments were though on.

Although I believed the dream have end up actual, it become impossible to create any give up end result that would permit me to attach the dream with reality. According to theories, our mind creates worlds similar to the simplest we sleep in at the same time as we experience an out-of-body enjoy. Many times, there can be a portal. Literally, it's miles a window or door within the dream that we are capable of go through to go into a completely unique world.

Although it is not stated why those dreams seem greater real than unique varieties of lucid or lucid dreams, it is viable that the mind area that offers with prolonged-term recollections and reason remains lively throughout sleep. One idea is that dreams may be interconnected with an exchange fact or shape of fact, known as the astral. No count number variety what the purpose, many folks that experience out-of-frame activities furthermore experience vibrations and feature auditory and visual hallucinations.

AWARENESS

THE ROUTE TO THE "BEYOND".

Being aware of dreaming can advise many stuff to considered certainly one of a kind humans. It is every so often called lucid dreaming.

When a dreamer reaches a high quality diploma of popularity in a dream nation, they will consider themselves to have had an "out-of-frame" revel in. Some people describe themselves as aware at the equal time as visiting via a variety of realities beyond the recognized senses of time in an astral united states. What is the boundary amongst waking fact, passive dreaming, and lucid dreaming?

These differences can best be made if we first apprehend cognizance. What exactly is reputation? What is interest and the way is it one-of-a-kind from the mind? These requirements must be understood that allows you to discover altered dream states in a large way.

In the medical network, research on consciousness is a novelty. Until lately, it changed into difficult to understand recognition. We will be inclined to confuse recognition with idea due to the reality we perceive it as such. That is why we neglect about the ambiguity of lucid dreaming or extraordinary approaches of exploring the beyond our thoughts: focus is a physical phenomenon.

Consciousness manifests as reputation, alertness and interest. These states may be professional internally and might most effective be professional by using using one man or woman. They are only evidenced externally through the behavior they produce. This is sufficient for practical features.

This is a instead intense implication. If attention can not be externally expert or tested, then my pleasant fact approximately my non-public cognizance is that it is not viable for me to understand the reality. I cannot be superb of some issue beyond that. I do no longer recognize if you, the reader, are conscious. I can handiest offer the benefit of the doubt.

Current theories at the origins and evolution of recognition cognizance on each the observer and the positioned. Tony Nader is a neuroscientist and researcher who's moreover a leader in Transcendental Meditation. He believes that to be conscious, some aspect must have essential characteristics.

Must be able to check.

He want to have seen himself.It's essentially a fowl and egg problem. To be aware about myself, I first want to take a look at myself or my awareness. To be aware, but, I ought to first be conscious to phrase and feature a have a look at my interest.

CONSCIOUSNESS IS PHYSICAL

Many philosophical and summary strategies to consciousness display the manner it develops in the thoughts and in our surroundings. These techniques are simplest one view of ways recognition can explicit itself. The bodily method to know-how focus is extra vital than the philosophical and abstract ones. It can screen masses about how consciousness arose and what it takes to enjoy it. Our facts of recognition draws on the physiological and organic basis of recognition in techniques that are as awesome as they'll be surprising.

The human thoughts gets sensory facts in 250 milliseconds. On commonplace, it takes 30 to 50 milliseconds to deliver stimuli to the mind, located by way of one hundred fifty milliseconds to machine them earlier than they advantage our attention. The everyday activation of synapses, additionally called cognition, is what we name cognizance. Neuroscientists and philosophers disagree on whether or not or no longer this is much like recognition or cognition.

Although it may appear that this is an automated manner and that we are sincerely experiencing what it's miles, what's definitely taking place backstage is greater like a computer display strolling at sixty frames constant with 2d, giving us the illusion of seeing a non-stop image.

The proof that physical reports should have an effect on awareness is overwhelming. Changes in how the frame abilties, which includes what you eat, what you drink and what you do with it, together with bodily trauma and strain, can purpose hormonal changes that result in reactions within the thoughts which might be then professional as focus.

The contrary is real: interest can have an effect on physical states. As the vintage announcing goes, change the manner you word and the belongings you word will trade. Many worldwide traditions recollect that trade starts offevolved with the spirit. Then the thoughts methods the information to create the responses within the body. This perception is supported through many cultures, each historical and current-day. The identical is real these days if we substitute the word spirit for attention. Changes in attention can regulate the hormonal balances inside the mind, which in flip affects the complete body.

Studying attention can be described as reading a map made with magic ink. When the hidden photograph is illuminated, its hidden which means that is observed out. The brain's oxygen consumption may be used as a biomarker to help researchers have a observe interest. If the brain consumes greater oxygen in certain areas, it approach that those areas have turn out to be more lively. This evaluation famous that distinctive regions of the thoughts are concerned in one-of-a-type obligations, and that awareness relies upon on many elements.

Although we can't see popularity, we're able to study neural hobby and oxygen used by the thoughts in a manner that indicates that popularity is happening. We can recognize patterns in neural interest and start to recognize the person of cognizance.

It is important to undergo in thoughts that reputation does now not communicate to the mind, the senses or a particular u . S . A . Of recognition. External elements, including the functioning of our thoughts and senses, can also have an impact on our popularity or the thoughts or perceptions we make. We can adjust recognition relying on how we interact with our senses, how our mind skills, or how we exchange our america of recognition, but popularity is a part unto itself, self-contained as a country of cognizance that is grew to become on at the same time as conscious or have come to be off whilst subconscious.

Understanding the ways wherein outside forces can alter cognizance is only part of records its malleability. How things are learned changes the improvement of hobby. We speedy soak up new topics and skills even as we first studies them. Learning takes location within the conscious thoughts. After information is processed, it's far stored in memory. This memory lives in our unconscious. This is referred to as implicit cognition. Implicit memory is a aggregate of cognition, perception and reminiscence. It impacts conduct but is not conscious. A conventional instance of implicit cognition is that we do not forget the way to trip a bicycle. The memory of the approach is stored inside the once more of our mind, so at the same time as we start driving, reminiscences of the frame mechanically come to the fore.

STATES OF CONSCIOUSNESS

There are three states of consciousness that can be located in clearly every body:

Awake: You are extensive awake, alert, cell and engaged to your each day sports activities activities.

Dreaming: You are maximum likely experiencing REM sleep. You can also moreover have a dream or a simulated reality enjoy in the end of sleep.

Deep sleep: While you aren't huge wakeful or dreaming, deep sleep allows you to be aware of thoughts and experience lucid. Deep sleep can purpose sleep paralysis, further to one-of-a-kind out-of-frame reviews.

In every of the states, an impairment may additionally additionally arise in which attention does now not feature properly or collapses. This does not endorse that the individual is unconscious or conscious. It most effective means that there is an altered usa of the usa of reputation that capabilities otherwise than may be expected even as simply aware. Below are a few examples of altered states.

Anesthesia is while a person is quickly subconscious and is given a chemical substance that causes his or her thoughts to enter a sleep kingdom.

The state of being locked in: Total paralysis of the body that makes one now not capable of transport. This is even as the individual feels trapped in his or her body. It is just like sleep paralysis, or unique paralysis research in which the man or woman is aware of sensations.

Minimally conscious: Although the mind stays able to responding to a few stimuli, it is not in a country of whole attention.

Vegetative u.S. Of america: A person is absolutely unresponsive (as although dead). This sleep united states of america is similar to an character's wakefulness.

Coma: An man or woman is not able to revel in the cycles of waking, dozing or dreaming. He is locked right into a single u . S . Of being that is an entire lot plenty much less conscious than his minimally aware country.

There are many styles of altered states of attention, that could result in attention in special tactics. Here are a few examples of the reviews one need to have at the equal time as in altered states of recognition:

Drug-added on hypnotic opinions: When fine hallucinogenic tablets are administered, thoughts functioning may be altered to create tremendous states of recognition. Perceptions, idea styles and feelings can be extensively altered in comparison to what is skilled at the same time as no longer the use of the drug. However, this does not necessarily mean that the man or woman is subconscious. Many instances, the patron can preserve whole interest even at the same time as the usage of those substances.

Lucid goals: A man or woman can experience lucid goals whilst they're asleep. This is once they emerge as aware that they'll be dreaming. This does no longer usually recommend that the dreamer enters the dream. However, it's far feasible that he or she does.

Sleepwalking: Although not often remembered, an individual may be aware that he or she can circulate in a snooze u.S.A..

Hypnosis is a country of focus wherein the person is capable of see outdoor influences and remains conscious.

As you could see, awareness can exchange in the course of the day. It's not quite a extraordinary deal how conscious we're, but moreover approximately how we recognize our fact and engage at a fundamental diploma with it. Interestingly, our attention is straight away related to how our frame reacts to the arena spherical it, together with our sleep cycles.

Chapter 2: Modulation Of Learning And Brain Awareness

Certain regions of the thoughts apprehend and manner outdoor stimuli. This statistics is processed to create a reality that makes revel in. Reality isn't always what we absolutely see. We handiest apprehend a processed and tailor-made representation of the statistics. It can take in to 1 / 4 of a 2nd earlier than we're privy to what we see. Before we end up privy to facts, a few regions of the thoughts understand it first. Consciousness most effective happens at the same time as every other vicinity of the mind becomes aware about the facts.

The a part of the mind responsible for regulating wakefulness is referred to as the reticular formation. This area additionally controls consciousness. Damage to it is able to cause coma. The reticular formation receives all sensory statistics earlier than it's miles processed with the useful resource of way of other elements of the thoughts. The brain additionally has one-of-a-type areas which is probably liable for precise factors of interest. The primary physical features that alter homeostasis are managed by means of using the hypothalamus. The middle of the self, or what we understand because the ego, is managed by means of the use of the amygdala and the midbrain. The cortex, additionally known as the autobiographical self or autobiographical self, is language, speech and memory.

The mind creates a simulation of the non-stop fact developing a protective impact. This is due to the fact the mind takes time to approach all of the records. The thoughts creates facts from what it can't advantage from the environment to offer us a non-stop enjoy in popularity. Individuals with superb mind illnesses or lesions might also additionally moreover enjoy a cinematic view of time that slows down and characteristic moments of belief in region of a non-stop go with the waft. This loss of time also can be because of various factors, collectively with mind damage or annoying activities.

The unconscious mind preprocesses the aware revel in we've got at some degree within the day (facts we aren't however aware of), so there may be continuously an element of ourselves that is not evident. This unconscious place controls an critical part of our experience. Lucid dreaming is even as we actively attempt to be aware of what we are seeing. If the subconscious mind does not need us to emerge as privy to the desires, we are able to in no way have the potential to perform that. Lucid dreaming strategies create a relationship with the unconscious to end up more privy to the unconscious fabric in desires.

CONSCIOUSNESS IS PSYCHOSPIRITUAL

Another element of interest is having an ego, or a revel in of self, that takes place inside the history. Even if you don't bear in mind who or what you are as a person, attention is responsible for shaping yourself-idea. The same self-generated attention is evident in how we define ourselves. For instance, identity, form, nationality or fame.

Real recognition, which extends beyond the experience of self and is essential to your popular view of fact, is each unique detail of interest. Real reputation is your thoughts, feelings, plans, desires, intentions, desires and emotions. These are your actions, or the manner you appear what you want most. Real interest is not tied to who you are as an man or woman. Instead, it is an expression and manifestation of what the Self most goals.

The vital issue to preserve in mind is that your revel in of self (or ego) is simplest part of who you genuinely are. There are additives of you which you do now not realize which is probably crucial for your dream revel in. You are much more likely to awaken to the deeper factors of your self if you may create a communicate between them. It is often a exquisite deal better to allow the unconscious guide us into interest in a dream than to stress it. The subconscious is what controls the dream international. The subconscious is what leads us to lucidity. It brings the unconscious cloth to hobby.

CONSCIOUSNESS IS A PHILOSOPHY

Although the terminology used to explain interest can also additionally moreover trade relying on how others outline it, in cutting-edge the capability to be huge wide awake and aware, in addition to the functionality to evaluate the environment, are the most important components of being conscious. Understanding that I am succesful and capable of examine the environment is an important problem of interest is critical. Unconsciously, I may be privy to some element however not be able to consciously compare it.

What is the problem of all this? These thoughts are the cornerstones of lucid dreaming. And because of the fact interest isn't always like wakefulness, we are capable of enjoy empowered and capable of explore our dream worlds. Being wide unsleeping, alert and attentive even on the equal time as slumbering enhances the potential to lucid dream.

On the opportunity hand, the unconscious in reality consists of the whole lot that is not conscious, but influences the aware thoughts. The subconscious consists of thoughts collectively with early reviews that have triggered the persona and forgotten memories. These are not usually to be had for inspection. Some of these memories can be accessed via changing our reputation. Some of those memories can be accessed with the aid of converting our interest.

The Unconscious does not exist within the mind; the aware is most effective privy to what the unconscious is privy to.

-FRENCH JEFFREY

The unconscious isn't itself unconscious. We are in truth now not aware of it. Only we are capable of realize that there may be something internal us of which we are unaware. However, the fact that we are consciously aware about something does now not propose that we aren't similarly or greater aware about it unconsciously. Carl G. Jung, a former student of Freud, and ostensibly the unique so-called intensity psychologist, believed that the unconscious modified into extra energetic in shaping who we're. Jung believed that the unconscious changed into liable for our attention, our ego and our feel of self. It is crucial to understand that our unconscious is a part of the exploration of desires. Dream opinions can assist us deliver the unconscious into our aware mind. Lucid dreaming and dream evaluation permit us to interact with our subconscious to discover more approximately the symbols and archetypes in our goals, and to discover its desires and goals. Interacting with those archetypes leads us to a extra cognizance of our right self.

Someday we are capable of understand how our brains have interaction with our senses and complexes to perceive the world round them. We can already understand human beings's mind the use of latest technologies whilst now not having to ask. Brain patterns may be used to decide what is going on inside the mind, with out the want to talk to the character. These styles may be diagnosed the use of positron emission tomography (PET scanning). Although the technology is still very primitive, it is promising.

Researchers are notwithstanding the fact that searching for to figure out what makes attention real. Is it feasible to recreate attention? How are we able to apprehend the subjective opinions all of us have? How are we able to recognize our personal experience nearly about that of others? No one knows the answer.

However, it seems obvious that imagination is part of subjective revel in. The power of creativeness is what makes attention and self-attention possible. It is feasible to evoke to our dreams the usage of imagination.

Awareness

How to prepare your dream

At first look, it might seem that lucid dreaming is a pretty clean capability to understand. All we have to do to have a lucid imaginative and prescient is virtually to dream. How are we able to benefit it? It is as clean as expertise the variations amongst dreaming and fact. However, that may be a tough assignment for most humans. Why? Why? Because our capacity to make rational observations can be very restrained in our dream country. It is important to growth the potential to lucid dream with the aid of being aware of your environment at some stage in the day.

It appears that by using developing our awareness at some stage in the day, we are able to increase our awareness for the duration of desires. This will make it less complex to comprehend that we are dreaming. Let's have a test this.

WHAT IS AWARENESS?

I regularly find out myself zoning out at a few level inside the day. I can pressure round town and arrive at my excursion spot, not even expertise how or what I emerge as paying attention to on the radio. This takes place because of the truth my mind is in a trance-like state, which I take into account is to address boredom while the usage of. It is also viable to song out to avoid uninteresting or everyday sports activities. We all enjoy the ones moments of absent-mindedness generally a day.

While it can appear alarming to suppose that we are all in a trance, there are a few blessings. It doesn't recommend we want to be focused on the subjects we do not like and we're capable of skip some different vicinity whilst doing the ones obligations. We can also break out and plan matters that won't be within the the the front of our eyes, or have mini-adventures and fantasies at the equal time as concentrating.

However, this u . S . Has a few drawbacks. One of them is that we lose sight of the essential things spherical us. Apart from the obvious dangers, which includes the opportunity of entering into an accident whilst the usage of, we are also not able to take note of all or a part of what is going on within the moment. It is feasible to disconnect from the actual international. This may be useful in powerful conditions, which include trauma, but in normal life, those intervals of desensitization can cause us to overlook the most crucial topics.

Lucid dreaming and the attention practices that useful resource it could assist us acquire the opportunity of dissociation. We are extra worried, conscious and in a position to take part in our lives at the equal time as wide awake, further to on the same time as dreaming.

Our capability to speak with the unconscious improves as we come to be extra aware and concerned in our each day lives. The subconscious can display us symbolic photographs and messages that we are capable of recognize. The unconscious can take over within the dream area, inflicting our awareness to go into a symbolic international that is normally unknown to us. If we do not exercising recognition schooling to grow to be more aware about this transition, we turns into genuinely absorbed via the subconscious international and lose sight of what we're truely dreaming.

MINDFULNESS

Mindfulness is one of the pleasant techniques to teach the mind for lucid dreaming. It's no wonder that of the arena's oldest lucid dreaming traditions, Egypt and Tibet, furthermore have the maximum huge mindfulness and meditation practices.

Modern studies has proven this connection: Researchers positioned a incredible correlation in lucid dreamers who have been able to lucid dream and those who had practiced mindfulness training.

Consciousness method to be conscious. It is the act of being attentive to what you are proper away aware of, so that you can see what is real. Mindfulness training is exactly this. Mindfulness schooling is the exercise and paintings of paying attention to the prevailing 2nd. It permits you to pay greater hobby to what also can seem normal, in addition to educate your mind to be more bendy. Mindfulness exercise will growth your capability to be aware about some thing you select.

What makes Mindfulness paintings?

Mindfulness schooling improves mind connections. The thoughts creates neural connections while we attention our hobby on an item or idea. The thoughts's potential to exchange suggests that it improves its capability to gadget information associated with what it considers important. This is each distinctive instance of the thoughts's excellent adaptive abilties.

The frame can also gain from mindfulness. The frame is an digital and chemical conversation device. The brain sends electric impulses to the frame, which are then transferred to the nerves. These chemical signals can then adventure to other nerves. These electric and chemical indicators come to be being translated into motion of a part of your frame. Some people accept as genuine with that the gaps among the nerves may also furthermore shop chemical materials. These gaps also can be answerable for trauma, ache or one of a kind ailments. If we attention on particular areas of the body, we're capable of direct electric powered and chemical impulses to those areas. This will beautify sign transmission and boom the thoughts's attention of these components. This permit you to release any trauma or pain that is stored for your frame.

HOW TO PRACTICE MINDFULNESS

There are strategies of mindfulness that can be especially useful in making prepared for lucid dreaming. The first is mindfulness meditation. Another is fact checking. Let's take a look at each.

Mindfulness meditation

Mindfulness meditation goals to prevent questioning. This allows electricity commonly spent on busy thinking to be directed in the direction of recognition. People mistakenly consider that the purpose of mindfulness meditation is to haven't any mind. This is incorrect. Mindfulness meditation asks that we allow mind to unfold and be open to just accept any remarks. Over time, your mind will discover ways to be a good deal much less connected to wandering mind by way of practising non-attachment.

Traditional mindfulness meditation includes mendacity down skip-legged along aspect your again straight away and snug. The intellectual manner is in fact to permit thoughts and feelings spread as you take a look at them. You need to now not pressure your mind or select them. Be aware of your mind and permit them to go with the flow.

Reality test

Reality checking can be considered a simple form of lucid dreaming. This exercising is a clean way to ask your self if the dream is real. However, it requires a few steps.

Be aware about your surroundings. This way being aware of your surroundings, together with the smells and experience of devices. Cell telephones, watches, and your arms are actual examples of gadgets you could recognition on.

Next, popularity on the item you've got selected and look for any strangeness. Then ask yourself, "Am I dreaming?". This is much like reciting a mantra. It is a repetition of words that brings recognition.

These kinds of reality checks need to be finished regularly sufficient so you can appearance intently on the objects to your dreams and ask yourself, "Am I dreaming?" Just as you do within the waking realm. You will frequently word uncommon homes in goals if you take note of items intently. For instance, your hand can also have seven arms in area of five. This will assist you recognise that you are truely asleep and dreaming.

This technique may be greater proper with the aid of identifying the versions among dream and waking reality right away after waking from a dream. Observe the desires you've got got have been given had, which encompass sounds, photographs, and physical sensations. Compare them to the actual global. You can advantage a higher level of reputation in both the waking and dream u . S . A . In case you get into the dependancy of comparing the dream worldwide with the actual worldwide.

QUALITY REST

Everyone merits a top notch night's sleep. We often wake up exhausted. However, on occasion we do now not get to sleep at the same time as we preferred to, and we spend the night time worrying or reeling from ache or pain. This no longer only impacts our day, however additionally our capacity and memory to don't forget our desires. These talents are essential for lucid dreaming. Lucid dreaming is simplest viable with a very good night time's sleep.

POOR SLEEP CAN HAVE NEGATIVE EFFECTS

Quality sleep can every now and then be interrupted via strain and the complications of regular existence. Our mind produces chemical modifications that may have an effect on reminiscence and cognition, in addition to hormones that affect weight, weight-reduction plan and mood. These effects may be noted in greater element even as we communicate memory and dream hold in thoughts in a later financial ruin. The U.S. Navy recognizes the significance of appropriate sleep and has made it compulsory for all protection pressure to get a positive sort of hours of sleep.

IMPROVE YOUR SLEEP: FIRST-HAND EXPERIENCE

In the navy I learned approximately the terrible effects of sleep deprivation and techniques to enhance sleep. In a sea of chaos, I labored lengthy hours on a Navy deliver. The paintings was demanding all day extended. Also, on a deliver there is lots of system and personnel running around the clock. The deliver's weapons system made me enjoy my chest throbbing, and I would awaken among one and three within the morning.

A Navy deployment can last up to 12 months. Poor sleep can cause extreme mental and bodily troubles. Sleep disruptions can bring about depression, aggression, confusion and weight advantage. Ferdinand Zizi and his research accomplice positioned that poor sleep can boom the hazard of growing diabetes. For a healthful mind and frame, it is critical to get correct, satisfactory sleep.

Good sleep conduct are like gaining knowledge of a modern-day device. It takes practice. Your sleep will decorate if you are affected person and curious to discover the extraordinary equipment for you and characteristic the perseverance to be normal. You will experience more conscious, be extra inexperienced at night time and characteristic a better reminiscence for your every day lifestyles and dreams. It is crucial to enlarge those property via installing region healthy sleep habits all through the day and night time.

I changed into in a function to analyze a few very useful techniques at the same time as doing my military provider. I genuinely have persisted to apply them on the same time as pursuing my dream career. These strategies may be divided into 3 instructions: each day behavior together with exercising and nutrients, further to dietary dietary supplements needed to assist relaxation and sleep.

DAILY HABITS TO PROMOTE SLEEP

What form of day must make you feel tired on the give up of the day? A day that includes plenty of exercising, balanced nutrients and stimulating intellectual pastime. It moreover includes wholesome manage of emotions. These are the tips I've decided out through trial and errors. They also can assist you broaden your private sleep-selling conduct.

Being exhausted

New dad and mom, tourists, military personnel and all of us who works long hours or has a demanding activity may additionally additionally tell you that being worn-out should make it hard to doze off speedy. This is because of the truth strain can cause insomnia. Regular workout can assist lessen cortisol tiers, which in turn allows the frame and thoughts to relax, permitting you to sleep higher. Cortisol (additionally known as the pressure hormone) is without delay associated with sleep regulation and our circadian rhythm abilities. You will sleep better if you reduce the amount of cortisol that is gift all through sleep.

Exercise

Regardless of your health degree, an wonderful exercise will will allow you to sleep higher with the resource of creating your frame and mind bodily exhausted. Exercise can also relieve strain and assist you fear much less approximately your day. Although there can be an lousy lot medical speak about the results of exercising on sleep, it is easy that exercise enables you doze off faster and sleep higher. Light yoga is a terrific opportunity in advance than bedtime. It entails deep respiration and stretching, which permit you to loosen up and fall asleep.

Diet

It is broadly identified that tryptophan may be a excellent sleep food, just like Thanksgiving turkey. Because tryptophan will boom degrees of acetylcholine, that's an vital neurotransmitter for sleep. Serotonin and GABA are also actual for sleep. GABA, tryptophan and seeds are meals that comprise tryptophan. It is important to eat more of these meals in some unspecified time in the future of the day and keep away from ingesting some issue before bedtime. Eating healthy materials also can make a contribution to outstanding sleep.

While deployed within the army or on the battlefield, I frequently couldn't have healthy, scrumptious meals or make my very personal alternatives. I needed to make do with what I had, even as improving the superb of my sleep in exclusive techniques. I have become capable of discover nutrients and special supplements that made up the distinction.

Supplements

You can use nutritional dietary supplements in aggregate with one of a kind techniques that will help you turn out to be greater conscious and conscious at the equal time as you sleep. Supplements will let you sleep higher, at the same time as others will make you greater conscious and alert all through sleep, growing your probabilities of waking up in a dream. Although some people keep in mind nutritional supplements to be a hoax for reaching lucid states of interest, many spiritual and religious traditions have used dietary supplements and herbs. Today, many components lack the vitamins had to manual natural sleep. Supplements can assist your frame collect natural sleep states.

Melatonin is my sleep aid to help me get to bed on time. Melatonin is produced glaringly through the brain. It can be taken as a supplement that will help you doze off.

Niacin is my preferred complement. It releases serotonin and a protein referred to as prostaglandin D2 (PGD2), that could be a snooze modulator. This helps us fall asleep.

Also extremely good sleep aids are five-Hydroxytryptophan (five-HTP), cautiously associated with serotonin, and St. John's Wort. They are moderate antidepressants that assist relax the mind and prepare for sleep.

Remember that nutrients and dietary dietary supplements want to handiest be used on the side of your medical physician's approval. They can pose a threat if now not used effectively. These and special dietary dietary supplements may be discussed in greater detail in Part 5.

You also can lessen the quantity of caffeine you eat for the duration of the day to get an outstanding night time time's sleep. It sounds no longer feasible, but it's far viable. I lessen out coffee and strength liquids for a few months while serving inside the Navy. This appreciably superior the top notch of my sleep, my stamina and my ordinary fitness.

Chapter 3: A Route To Bed To Promote Good Sleep

Even in case your regular has improved your probabilities of getting an remarkable night time time time's sleep, it's how you method bedtime so one can determine your achievement. This is what devices the level in your dreams. You have to attend to your inner and out of doors environment so as to have a healthy sleep cycle and exercise having a pipe dream.

For your thoughts, create a stable vicinity for sound asleep

How the unconscious works and what it is remains under debate. It appears that there are minds in our thoughts. As we referred to in advance, the conscious mind is what we assume with each day. It is likewise what we've in thoughts when we consider our identification. The subconscious thoughts isn't part of our each day popularity. It thinks generally approximately survival. The subconscious is involved with preserving us safe and steady. It attracts our hobby to what it thinks will maintain us stable and steady. Sometimes which means that that the subconscious keeps us massive unsleeping, in spite of the fact that our aware thoughts want to be asleep.

Perhaps you're pressured and your unconscious is detecting a threat which you can not defuse. Perhaps your creativeness is developing horrifying memories, gambling "what if" video video games of possible futures, or maintaining you alert to actual or imagined threats. If this occurs, you can discover it tough to fall asleep at night time. You might not be actively involved about whatever, however the equal concerns are taking walks in your historic beyond. The unconscious does no longer distinguish. What's the answer?

How to calm the thoughts

A calm mind couldn't come from an area of "ifs" and "maybes." If your unconscious is sending you survival signs, it is time to talk to yourself, preserve a mag and get out of the rut.

Meditation and reputation training

Meditation teaches us that feelings and mind are regularly no longer as essential as we anticipate. Meditation lets in us to disconnect from our mind and quiet our busy minds to be extra effective in our lives. This consists of letting go of our mind at bedtime.

Having the communicate

If I lie down and my mind is racing, it takes me a while to doze off. That's on the identical time as it's time for The Talk. When I turn to my very very personal thoughts, I write (or say) this: You understand it is essential to get sufficient sleep. These are the topics which is probably bothering you proper now. List them. They aren't important proper now. They cannot be constant urgently. No. They may be regular the next day. We're secure till then. It's time to visit bed proper now.

This permits to calm the mind through spotting your thoughts. For the unconscious to understand, we want to speak or write first-rate terms.

The final a part of "The Talk" is robust. If I say "It's time for bed!" out loud, I regularly yawn, get worn-out and fall asleep. Talking to oneself is a form of meditation. Clearing the mind is the important detail to dreaming.

For the relaxation of your life, create a steady area for sleep

We set the level for our dreams by using the use of using getting organized for bed. This manner that your mattress room and bedding must be quiet and clean. Make sure the gap is as uncluttered and easy as feasible. Place devices in a manner that makes you experience happy and cushty. Surround yourself with scents and textures that soothe your senses without overwhelming them.

This is extra than developing a pleasing aesthetic. The aspect to don't forget is the subconscious. Its reason is to maintain your mind secure. Your mind can become indignant with litter, chaos and stress. Watch how an animal rests and arranges its bedding so it feels steady and stable. It's an remarkable detail.

Turn off the lighting

Put away your devices, too. Even if it makes you revel in higher to be huge awake at night time, your night time time slight isn't always helping you sleep. Even the smallest quantity of mild can forestall your thoughts from generating melatonin, the herbal sleep useful useful aid. Your sleep hygiene will enhance when you have a darkened bed room.

Better sleep for all

You can enhance your sleep regardless of your activity, life-style, place or stress degree. These tools assist you to attain a amazing sleep surroundings. While not always the remarkable, any improvement is a step inside the proper direction.

It want to be stated that I used these tools in the course of my military deployment. Although I had a few sleepless nights, I have to charge my normal sleep excellent as great. My capability to sleep higher advanced appreciably.

I count on so.

SLEEP PARALYSIS AND MEMORY

THE DOOR IS THE OBSTACLE

He lived by myself in an vintage residence in Virginia at the identical time as running as a military mechanic on the night shift. Due to the pressure of the time desk and constant paintings, I couldn't get as loads sleep as I preferred. My roommates may also make loud noises at some stage inside the day that might wake me from my ordinary sleep. Once, I belief my friend jumped on my over again and pinned my head to the mattress. Then, he started blowing in my ears. This disturbed me and made it even greater frightening. I could not flow into due to his superb electricity. His respiration intensified and made me skip more difficult.

I turned into eventually capable of unfastened myself and located out that I grow to be by myself. I have become asleep all the time and imagined everything.

I became terrified and started learning what had occurred. I spent months mastering and analyzing to find out what sleep paralysis changed into and why it have end up taking place to me. I moreover found out a manner to address it so I must face my fears and regain control of my goals.

While this isn't supposed to discourage truly all of us from dreaming, it may be frightening. Let's start with the hard component.

Lucid goals can lead many human beings to come across emotionally stressful challenge subjects and pictures. These horrifying photos are regularly observed thru using an disability to transport.

Sleep paralysis is a totally commonplace situation among lucid dreamers. You owe it to yourself to observe greater in advance than you leap in.

WHAT IS SLEEP PARALYSIS?

It is the u . S . As a innocent duration of immobility, deriving from muscle paralysis, or atonia that takes area each night time time time as a natural aspect impact of dream sleep. This information can help alleviate some of the anxiety that can be expert.

When our body falls asleep, but we're partly aware, this is called sleep paralysis. This is due to the fact the thoughts transitions from fast eye movement (REM) to non-speedy eye motion (NREM) sleep. The thoughts's transition from rapid eye motion (REM) to non-speedy eye motion (NREM) sleep regularly motives us to dream, however we are conscious that that is taking location. The give up quit result may be hallucinations, which also can encompass unwanted visitors or the sensation of being watched. Dreamers describe sleep paralysis as a experience of paralysis, the perception of a presence and the imaginative and prescient of terrifying creatures.

Although sleep paralysis can be frightening, it's miles everyday. Rubin Naiman, Ph.D., is a psychologist and clinical associate professor of medicine. He is also the sleep and dream expert at the Andrew Weil Center for Integrative Medicine at the University of Arizona. He confident me that, in spite of the fact that it is able to be frightening, "sleep paralysis" is absolutely normal. In truth, our frame immobilizes us on the identical time as we sleep simply so we do now not want to behave out our dreams. This is what can rise up if the mechanism fails. However, sleep paralysis isn't to be feared. Sleepwalking has been associated with mind protrusion, in accordance to analyze. Sam Kean stated, "Deep in the reptilian mind is the pons, a centimeter-lengthy hump within the mind stem. The hump sends signs to the primate mind thru which desires are initiated at the same time as we fall asleep. The pons sends messages to the spinal twine under it all through desires. This produces chemical compounds that numb the muscle groups. This transient paralysis prevents nightmares and escape from the mattress room.

Sleep paralysis is whilst we awaken and can hallucinate pix approximately our out of doors surroundings. It is just like an augmented fact for the brain.

People document feeling hectic and stressful once they nod off, no matter what they see or pay hobby. The cause can be hyperactivation of the amygdala, that is the priority middle of the thoughts. Sleep paralysis and amygdala activation might be the cause of nightmares or sleep paralysis.

WAYS TO PARTIALLY STOP SLEEPING

Researchers do no longer however understand why some humans enjoy paralysis and others do no longer. Research indicates that sleep paralysis can be extended if lucid dreaming strategies are used. Wake Back to Bed (WBTB), and Wake Induced Lucid Dreamings (WILD), lucid dreaming strategies that inspire practitioners to experience consequences just like or mimicking sleep paralysis.

There isn't any way to prevent sleep paralysis. However, there are a few matters you may do to reduce your threat.

Do now not sleep in your back

Sleeping in appeared locations.

Do not take naps for the duration of the day.

Get some workout in the course of the day.

Avoid stress earlier than bedtime.

Avoid stimulants on the equal time as slumbering.

To prevent mild from getting into your eyes, placed on a sleep masks.

Get a wonderful night time's sleep each night time time time.

Eat a healthy weight loss plan.

There are some topics you could do in case you revel in sleep paralysis.

Wiggle your arms and ft.

Relax your mind.

Deepen your respiration.

Think about turning. Close your eyes.

Talk in your doctor if you have any questions about sleep paralysis.

Ryan Hurd's ebook Sleep Paralysis - A Guide to Hypnagogic Visions, Night Visitors, that could be a complete e-book on the subject of sleep paralysis, covers plenty of these techniques.

THE POWER OF SLEEP PARALYSIS

Fear is a powerful tool. Fear should make us do exquisite subjects and moreover cause us to do terrifying topics. Fear can be used within the media, in advertising and advertising and advertising and marketing and in battle as a motivator, device or weapon. Sleep paralysis is a way of coping with the most scary reports we are able to recall, for people who are exploring their attention. It is feasible to practice going through and accepting our fears, further to eliminating their energy.

This fear is described in the Tibetan Book of the Dead due to the fact the father or mother of the door to the afterlife. Jung makes use of the archetypes of the shadow to explain this worry. Traditions as numerous as Christianity, Freemasonry and alchemy talk of overcoming the shadow via confronting the priority within the archetype of death. Although sleep paralysis may be distressing, it's far essential to take the hazard of lucid dreaming.

Chapter 4: Sleep Paralysis Seen From Another Perspective

It is critical to without a doubt acquire sleep paralysis. Accepting that the unknown is there and accepting the reality that we can't manage it can often be enough to cast off fear. Sleep paralysis can serve to determine if we're prepared to stand fear and distinct components of ourselves that we do no longer need or want to govern.

Imagine looking a frightening movie and abruptly know-how the entire film from beginning to stop. It might be truly as horrifying, and might even damage the fun. The same is going for sleep paralysis. Accepting that you're going to enjoy some thing regular, frightening and uncommon allow you to lessen the concern.

Sleep paralysis is a profound lesson for existence. How commonly in our lives will we react to what is taking place earlier than we are able to recognize it? Often that is due to fear, reluctance or fear of accepting statistics that isn't ours or that we can't manipulate. We exercise mediating the unknown in lucid dreaming and sleep paralysis. We may be extra compassionate in our every day lives if we are able to workout compassion for ourselves in our sleep.

You can also phrase at the same time as you dream which you are privy to your environment, this is called sleep paralysis. You can use this interest to set lucid dreaming in motion with the useful useful resource of truly allowing the dream to arise as you have a look at it. This view of sleep paralysis is one manner to release lucid dreaming, similarly to to free yourself from phantom worry.

MEMORY AND REM SLEEP

A regular individual goals approximately 4 or five times a night, and high-quality one or two dreams are retained. Some desires are simplest a short sound or a flash of slight. However, all are goals. Dreams are maximum not unusual in REM sleep. However, we can also dream all through NREM (or non-REM) sleep...

The tough element isn't dreaming, but remembering.

In this economic catastrophe we will communicate about memory and dream memory. We will even speak how goals can be used to beautify memory.

It is not stated how goals are remembered. There are many theories that each provide a bit of the puzzle. When we take them all together, we will discover clues to assist us keep in mind our goals. We can then growth practices to help this preserve in thoughts.

LONG-TERM EMPOWERMENT

Understanding how reminiscence works is essential to statistics dream reminiscence. Although this system is not but completely understood, one precept that has obtained reputation is long-term potentiation (or LTP). This happens on the same time as synapses, which may be the areas that be part of neurotransmitters to the brain, keep to hearth for a long term in a particular pattern. This activation motives a strengthening of the synapse with its neighboring synapses. This strengthens the synapse and creates a memory. On the alternative hand, state of no activity can cause lengthy-time period depletion (LTD) and weaken the links that exist among synapses and people spherical them.

Because of the significance of LTD in lengthy-time period memories, research on LTP has centered basically on the hippocampus. This is why it is critical for dreamers. Because the hippocampus performs a essential characteristic in goals, it converts quick-term recollections (the dream revel in) into prolonged-term memory in different areas of the thoughts. This permits us to keep in thoughts the dream when we awaken. The thoughts releases unique neurotransmitters and hormones that permit LTD or LTP inside the hippocampus. These chemical strategies are poorly understood. However, Dr. Allan

Hobson of Harvard Medical School, a psychiatrist who is moreover a dream researcher, has furnished greater notion into how dream memory works. We will speak it underneath.

ACTIVATION-SYNTHESIS HYPOTHESIS

During REM sleep, this is the volume whilst we have the most bright desires, there may be an growth in thoughts stages of the protein acetylcholine. This chemical performs a key function in strengthening synapses. Memory loss has been linked to Alzheimer's patients. This is due to the reality the mechanisms that produce acetylcholine have been destroyed. One feasible motive why we're able to keep in mind our goals is the boom in acetylcholine.

However, this concept has its limitations. Each of our sleep cycles lasts about ninety minutes. They also encompass the REM section. This increases many questions. If there are various sleep ranges in keeping with night time time and the REM section occurs in every segment, why is it so tough to undergo in thoughts every segment? This is why it's so hard to go through in thoughts goals early within the night time, or at the identical time as we aren't huge unsleeping after an REM section. It's not pretty much acetylcholine.

Although memory formation in desires will growth inside the REM stages of the night time time time and morning, this suggests that dreaming is a greater complex technique than truely supplying acetylcholine to the thoughts.

Glutamate, some other neurotransmitter underneath check for its role in reminiscence and its dating to Alzheimer's ailment, is also being investigated. GABA is also affected by glutamate, an excitatory neurotransmitter. Glutamate becomes a good deal much less energetic at the same time as hippocampal glutamate is lively. Research has shown that substances which consist of alcohol and marijuana can bind to GABA receptors within the hippocampus. This leads to a surprising end end result: the shortage of capability to create new reminiscences. The reminiscence of dreams may be restored if we permit those intoxicating substances disappear.

Glutamate and acetylcholine seem like the two fundamental culprits in the advent of new recollections. Research has furthermore shown that hormones are an critical part of this equation.

The pineal gland hormone oxytocin.

The pineal gland is associated with desires and adjusted states of popularity. This may be because it glaringly includes dimethyltryptamine in rats. The pineal gland, additionally called the 0.33 eye or the 0.33 eye, consists of hormones concerned within the sleep-wake tool, consisting of melatonin, vasotocin and oxytocin. Although little is understood approximately the feature of oxytocin in sleep, it has a first rate impact on memory and dreams.

When melatonin and oxytocin are released at some stage in sleep, REM sleep is activated. Oxytocin is also worried in modulating GABA and glutamate ranges within the hippocampus. This impacts the important disturbing machine. The pineal gland converts serotonin to melatonin and melatonin, and melatonin hobby is most inside the morning and reduces in the course of the night time. The balance of this oxytocin-melatonin-serotonin cocktail might also moreover make contributions to fluctuations in our capability to don't forget goals. Cortisol

Cortisol is each one of a kind trouble contributing to don't forget, however it's miles frequently unnoticed. Cortisol, like oxytocin and melatonin, additionally follows a circadian rhythm. It is involved in reminiscence formation in the hippocampus. Cortisol degrees which may be too immoderate can bring about hippocampal disease. This can bring about reminiscence problems.

Cortisol, a stress hormone, can be decreased through way of mindfulness meditation and workout. The hippocampus may be tormented by practices on the side of dream journaling and paying attention to binaural beats. Reality tests may have an impact on cortisol levels, which may additionally furthermore give an reason behind why they appear to beautify dream keep in mind.

A DREAM PILL?

Galantamine is a remedy regularly prescribed to Alzheimer's patients to offer some of the compounds had to improve reminiscence. Galantamine has been confirmed to be very powerful in improving reminiscence and lucid dreaming, in accordance to research courting once more to 2006. Galantamine can help humans come to be greater aware about their desires and manage them. It furthermore permits lucid dreaming. Galantamine's functionality to inhibit the enzyme acetylcholinesterase is what most researchers take transport of as real with is the purpose it is so powerful in enhancing don't forget. Acetylcholinesterase is accountable for the breakdown of acetylcholine. Studies have tested that reminiscence consider within the thoughts is right away related to acetylcholinesterase, so reducing acetylcholinesterase can also additionally moreover assist enhance memory formation. Galantamine will even growth thoughts glutamate, it truly is related to reminiscence formation. This makes it an extremely effective device for reminiscence enhancement.

Galantamine has had first rate consequences on me in my opinion. We will speak the feasible consequences and affects of galantamine in every one-of-a-kind chapter. However, it is vital that you seek advice from your physician in advance than taking any dietary dietary supplements to make certain they're regular.

BEYOND SIMULATION

What does it propose to be aware about dreaming? Just as there are many levels to focus, there also are many levels to lucid dreaming. It is nearly as if you are residing in a simulation. It simulates the truth that you see at the identical time as you're conscious. You do not understand you are in a simulation, however you experience it. A lucid dream is at the same time as you're conscious that you are inside the simulation.

Just as in a online game, whilst you switch out to be familiar with the simulation you'll be able to find out the controls and feature them. Over time, you will be in a function to overcome the simulation and speak at once with the goal psyche if you purchased more education and increase your reputation.

The first degree of lucid dreaming is in fact being aware which you are dreaming. More art work is wanted to maintain beyond this stage. This art work has been defined inside the literature on Buddhist dream yoga, Aristotle's description of being conscious in dreams, non secular artwork promoted and maintained by means of the Catholic Church, similarly to in contemporary-day clinical research. All of these resources offer maps to assist us triumph over the dream simulation created through our subconscious self and input into a completely unique form of dream revel in. One wherein we will have out-of-frame studies or astral projection. It is as lots as you the way a protracted way you go with lucid dreaming and what insights you advantage from it.

LET'S DO IT!

THE BASICS

It is normally pretty clean to have the primary sleep. Most dreamers collect it in a count variety of hours inside the occasion that they have a wholesome way of existence and an extremely good bedtime habitual.

There are almost as many lucid dreaming techniques as there are dreamers. This way that, in case you run into an obstacle, you've got got many options. This bankruptcy will cover the basics of lucid dreaming and provide some techniques to useful resource your dreams.

Lucid dreaming may be considered a exercise of cognizance. Anyone can do it. You don't should be a spiritual guru to do it. But, in case you do, congratulations! You clearly need to just accept as proper with that you can lucid dream after which determine to practice. By truely immersing yourself inside the thoughts of lucid dreaming, which include studying about it or talking about it, you may increase your probabilities of lucid dreaming.

There are numerous courses that promise lucid dreaming fulfillment. There are numerous publications that promise lucid dreaming fulfillment. However, few human beings agree at the excellent practices. Fewer despite the fact that are the strategies which may be best for maximum people. Here are seven easy steps to get you started out in your adventure to lucid dreaming.

SEVEN STEPS OF THE PROCESS

Good sleep hygiene and purpose setting are the ideas of lucid dreaming. This is the first step to lucid dreaming. Don't rush to investigate greater suggestions. You can be amazed how simple actions which includes noticing your surroundings, setting sleep intentions and supporting your dream can assist your mind wake up your very private potential.

These steps are a framework for lucid dreaming. These steps may be divided into 3 companies: earlier than, in the direction of and after dreaming. Each organisation gadgets the quantity for the subsequent. It will take approximately weeks to phrase adjustments on your functionality to keep in mind and be aware of your desires, and to experience lucid dreaming.

BEFORE GOING TO SLEEP

Reality take a look at: Perform truth assessments inside the course of the day.

Take examine of strategies matters enjoy, what food tastes like, what your palms appear like and the manner you have interaction with them. This is because of the fact we frequently see subjects in dreams that don't in form our fact. Or which might be out of place. These mistakes can be the vital thing to attaining lucidity. Ask your self this query throughout the day, "Am I dreaming?" If possible, say it out loud. Next, make the effort to keep in mind what you are wondering. Ask yourself the question and then have a have a look at your waking environment to find out why. To assist you understand in case you are dreaming, you may use truth checks to have a look at your waking environment.

Alarm: Your alarm ought to burst off 4 to six hours after waking from sleep. Your frame and thoughts must be properly rested earlier than trying to lucid dream. Your REM cycles will very last longer the greater sleep cycles you've got got. Each sleep cycle lasts approximately ninety mins. Since the REM phase is associated with dreaming, it's miles believed that the longer the REM cycle, the more the possibilities of having a dream or becoming lucid.

Your reason: Say that you will have a lucid vision. You can inform your self that your goals can be remembered and that dreams are important.

DURING SLEEP

Get up in advance than the alarm is going off.

Relax and get equipped for sleep. Get used to dreaming lucidly.

Go back to sleep: This is the toughest thing. You can be overstimulated and having trouble falling asleep. Relax and forget approximately about everything. You will discover that your thoughts will awaken surely at the same time as you begin this new ordinary and you will be capable of fall yet again to sleep pretty often. Your frame will experience a snooze phase each hour, after which you can wake up. Try not to transport or open your eyes currently. Although you need to be conscious which you are awake, try to take into account yourself in the relaxation room reflect or visualize a face or item on your head. If possible, do not pass. But consider your body shifting for your thoughts. It does no longer recall in case you do now not skip, it's far top enough. You can be capable of strive many things in advance than you get up and start your day. All you need to do is relax and allow the enjoy spread. It will show up. If you preserve in thoughts a dream, you could reputation your interest on it and recollect your self inside the dream. Then keep in mind what you may have finished if you have been lucid. As if you have been lucid, recollect the dream and make the aim to lucid dream even as you are lower decrease back in mattress.

AFTER DREAMING

Participate: Whether you lucid dream or no longer, having conversations with distinct lucid dreamers will assist you reap the subsequent degree.

REMEMBERING YOUR DREAMS

As I truly have stated in advance than, remembering your dreams is the maximum vital component in lucid dreaming. Although we may also moreover have lucid desires every night time time, you are not possibly to consider them. ....

Hobson, the Harvard dream researcher, claims that the hippocampus (the region of the brain that controls long-term reminiscences) shuts down whilst we dream. Although we can do not forget factors of our dreams, we often neglect them as soon as we wake up. We may also moreover have many dreams in a single night time time. Many of those dreams we do now not understand we've got got had because we shut down.

There are many techniques that can be used to triumph over this trouble and boom the possibilities of remembering desires. These thoughts had been clarified and improved by way of me. I really have additionally classified them steady with their complexity and type. These are the fundamentals, beginning with the basics and finishing with superior tools for folks that can not sleep well sufficient to attain lucidity. In the following chapters, we will look at a number of those techniques in extra element.

EASY

Exploring the degree and environment

Set and putting is a time period that comes from the lexicon of psychoactive drugs. Onirologists, who take a look at dreams, have determined it because of the truth the dream revel in is much like a psychedelic excursion. David Jay Brown explores the connection among lucid desires and psychedelics in Dreaming Wide Awake. Set and setting is a concept that includes listening to your environment and developing an environment that permits you to have super stories. This concept can also be done to lucid dreaming.

Take a go searching your mattress room to appearance what your environment looks like. Does it enjoy like a place in which you can dream and sleep? Is it just a collection of disorienting gadgets? Clear out the litter and electronic devices. The pineal gland, this is photosensitive, will produce melatonin if you preserve the lighting fixtures off.

Configuration and adjustment moreover encompass the way you function yourself in mattress. Body function may also have an impact at the wonderful of lucid dreams. For instance, mendacity on your stomach may additionally result in greater commonplace desires, even as mendacity for your returned can also moreover produce greater out-of-frame lucid desires.

Chapter 5: Keeping A Dream Diary

A dream mag is the maximum important device to your lucid dreaming toolbox. Keep your lengthy-term memory energetic with dream journals. Keeping a magazine can increase our functionality to recollect and hold dreams after waking up. Because it includes a mixture of thoughts, senses and motion, the physical act of writing terms and pix in a magazine can also have an effect on recognition.

USE A SLEEP MASK

A sleep masks is critical for dreaming in case you do no longer sleep in complete darkness. A sleep mask now not first-rate gives the darkness wished for great goals, but additionally serves as a fact test. If you can see surely and go to bed with the masks on, you'll recognize you're dreaming.

MEDITATION AND AWARENESS

It is essential to be privy to what you're doing each day to reach lucidity. Being privy to what you're doing in every second lets in you to interest on the winning and allows you to dream. Meditation is a first rate way to smooth your thoughts. Focus for your breathing and meditate. Concentrating on a particular object or to your breathing is a extraordinary way to growth dream hold in mind and decorate your chances of turning into lucid.

TO BE AWARE OF SLEEP PROCESSES

It is vital to understand what your body does earlier than you go to sleep. This will help you recognize and show the changes that stand up as you fall asleep. As your frame falls asleep, you may enjoy body spasms, temperature fluctuations, visible and auditory hallucinations, further to specific physiological reactions. Practice gazing your particular technique. You also can set and modify your body to result in a slightly lower body temperature. This will motive your frame's sleep cycles. You can boom your focus with the aid of way of the use of lying for your lower again and training breathing strategies.

Using MILD

Mnemonic Induced Lucid Dreaming (MILD) is one of the quality techniques to don't forget topics and increase your lucid dreaming capability. Numerous research have validated that MILD is one of the great methods to increase your probabilities of lucid dreaming. Learn extra approximately MILD in Chapter nine.

INTERMEDIATE

Get up and bypass!

Although it may appear counterintuitive, waking up regularly can train your thoughts to trade among being wakeful (the kingdom most related to cognizance) or asleep (the u . S . A . Maximum associated with dreams). You might also furthermore wake up more often than you ought to, that might alter your sleep cycle and make your mind more alert on the equal time as you must be snoozing. This will decorate your consider of desires and your commonplace manipulate over them.

Avoid alcohol

Your dreams may be suffering from what you eat and drink. People revel in a few beverages within the nighttime. Drinking is a popular way to loosen up and assist you sleep. There is a few reality to the idea that alcohol, even in huge portions, can growth the style of dreams and reminiscences you have got. This is due to the reality alcohol can boom the quantity of serotonin to your tool. You might also consider that serotonin blocks REM sleep and GABA decreases reminiscence formation. Once serotonin ranges drop, there may be a rebound from REM segment, that is an extended REM duration than commonplace. GABA ranges drop and long-term reminiscence formation appears amplified.

Although REM rebound might also moreover sound like a first rate manner to do not forget lucid dream sequences, the long-term terrible fitness effects of alcohol use for lucid dream induction (together with lack of serotonin over time and reduced sleep remarkable) are possibly to outweigh the benefits.

NATURAL WAYS TO INCREASE SEROTONIN

Drinking milk in advance than bedtime or eating fish will increase serotonin degrees. This can cause REM rebound. For comparable effects, you may additionally take five-HTP earlier than bedtime. It is a natural precursor of serotonin.

MODIFY YOUR SLEEP CYCLE

It's an super idea to mix up your exercise exercises if you need to assemble muscle. To have lucid goals, you want to additionally combination it up even as you visit bed. Your body and mind will start to apprehend whilst it is regular that lets in you to doze off. You can trick your mind via converting the times you visit bed and awaken, so that you can make it anticipate you're conscious. This will assist you turn out to be extra aware about your desires.

TAKE INTO ACCOUNT THE SUPPLEMENTARY AID

Thomas Yuschak lists the severa dietary dietary supplements he tried to decorate his lucid dreaming in his e-book Advanced Lucid Dreaming. This exercise is typically referred to as Supplement-Induced Lucid Dreaming, which involves nutritional dietary supplements that reduce the quantity of REM inside the first half of of the night time time and boom REM later inside the sleep cycle. My personal experiments have established me that dietary dietary supplements that increase serotonin and acetylcholine manufacturing are the best for lucid dreaming.

Use caution. To ensure safety, you want to seek advice from your scientific clinical health practitioner earlier than taking any complement.

CAFFEINE

Caffeine-based stimulants, together with espresso and caffeine, can boom the producing of various chemical materials. For this cause, many human beings drink the ones liquids to awaken. Caffeine can help human beings go to sleep if taken in small doses. Caffeine acts as an adenosine antagonist and can assist the conversion of serotonin into melatonin by way of manner of using the pineal gland. The manner caffeine is consumed can be applied in lucid dreaming (see CWILD under).

Caffeine-introduced on lucid dreaming (CWILD)

This superior method uses caffeine to create an addiction. As intense as it sounds, this is the fact. Then the caffeine is suddenly removed. Withdrawal signs and symptoms and symptoms and signs and symptoms rise up and also you fall asleep. When you're in a REM state, you are more likely to awaken. These withdrawal symptoms and signs and symptoms and symptoms disappear and are a hallmark that the dreamer is in a dream.

SEROTONIN

Serotonin is chargeable for reducing REM segment and enhancing dream maintain in mind. It is also diagnosed to have daytime benefits: serotonin has been shown to lessen melancholy, enhance mood and decrease the choice to overeat. 5-HTP may be used to increase serotonin production.

ACETYLCOLINE

Acetylcholine, a neurotransmitter that aids reminiscence, is proper away associated with wakefulness degrees. The body can growth the volume of acetylcholine at the same time as dozing through the usage of the usage of choline salts. These salts promote the producing of the neurotransmitter acetylcholine. Galantamine, an acetylcholinesterase inhibitor, can be particularly effective because it prevents the everyday breakdown of acetylcholine and lets in it to accumulate inside the thoughts.

HISTAMINES

Although histamines are not regularly referred to inside the lucid dreaming community, they will be important. Histamines are a way of liberating serotonin within the body. Histamines also can release a protein called PGD2, it's idea to be chargeable for sleep arousal. If you are inclined to be anxious via the niacin impact, niacin (or diet B3) is a great supplement. Niacin can motive a pores and pores and skin reaction that releases serotonin, PGD2 and reasons a flushing of the pores and pores and skin. This is accompanied with the aid of fatigue and a sense of rest.

CHRONOMETER

It seems that having the right nutritional dietary supplements is half of of the battle. However, it's far equally important to apply them efficaciously. The Wake Back to Bed

(WBTB) approach is the splendid (see Chapter 10).

During the day: Take a caffeinated beverage or complement. This will result in a later withdrawal.

Daytime: Do now not eat caffeine the day in advance than you need to have a glittery sleep.

Take a aggregate of five-HTP and niacin earlier than bedtime. This will will let you have greater great desires and will also help you preserve in thoughts your goals later in the night time time after waking up.

Two hours after bedtime, awaken and supplement with galantamine collectively with some caffeine. This will enhance reminiscence and sleep cycle competence, further to growth REM rebound about four hours earlier than bedtime.

This approach need to not be used every night, or any night time you do no longer expect to get six hours of sleep.

DAILY RITUAL

It is critical to set up a each day exercising to have lucid desires in the course of the night time time. This manual will will assist you to be constant.

Supplements/Meditation: in advance than going to sleep, take a mixture of niacin and five-HTP nutritional dietary supplements. You can relax in meditative mode using a breathing technique that calms you and prepares you for sleep.

When you've got got finished meditating, doze off.

Wake up after hours of sleep. This will allow the frame to lucid dream and relaxation. Galantamine also can be taken upon awakening. Then you may wait one hour earlier than going back to sleep.

Meditation, improved REM sleep because of galantamine and a cushty us of a make it possible so as to have lucid desires of the WILD type.

Repeat steps C and D without extra galantamine to attempt more than one WILD desires. You can hold this machine until you are ready to start the next day.

Write down your dreams whilst you awaken. This will assist you reaffirm your lucid dreaming goals.

Additional meditations may be achieved inside the direction of the day that aren't associated with lucid dreaming, on the facet of mindfulness, frame interest meditations, and yoga practices. Alternate days some of the lucid dreaming practices defined in this ebook and the greater meditation practices.

Chapter 6: Lucid Dreaming: The Gentlest Form

Now which you have a number one overview of lucid dreaming, allow's amplify at the simplest techniques for attaining lucidity.

The dream beneath indicates that I had been training Lucid Dreaming for some nights every week. This turn out to be my first night time the use of the Mnemonic Induced Lucid Dreaming (MILD) technique. Although I become no longer lucid for extremely prolonged, it have become an tremendous revel in.

I am presently taking education in college, and I am having problem passing a number of them. These goals are commonplace for me, and I am currently in university taking education which can be out of my comfort zones. At one aspect, I understand I am dreaming and my whole body starts offevolved to go with the flow within the dream. The dream continues, however I rapid lose focus.

This revel in taught me that MILD can be a powerful tool if used correctly. Stephen LaBerge's peer-reviewed research discovered out that MILD can't only activate lucid dreaming, but also notably enhance the dreamers' ability to lucid dream.

Mnemonics are a commonplace memory method that you may have located out in college. It works because of the truth our brains find out it less complicated to take into account facts that has been visualized than to retrieve facts that is extra complicated and tough to visualise. That's why acronyms are much less difficult to undergo in mind than extended phrases. These equal techniques can be applied in lucid dreaming. I talk to them as memory bridges, which can be reference factors that link the sports activities of a dream to a familiar feeling, sound or event. These emotions, sounds and activities can without problems turn out to be visible memories.

LaBerge had research individuals awaken inside the nighttime to preserve in mind their dreams and then recollect what might also want to have befell inside the occasion that they've been lucid. Participants need to focus in this idea after which pass lower returned to mattress with the motive of getting a lucid night time time time. They might also take into account their beyond goals as even though they were lucid. This reminiscence manner allowed the dreamers to be lucid in the next dream with the aid of developing the mnemonic pattern that our thoughts craves.

HOW TO DO IT

Here is a short summary of the MILD method.

You can nod off with the cause of having a lucid dream.

Stand up and live your dream.

As if you have been having lucid goals, consider the dream you without a doubt had. Imagine what you'll do if it were a lucid dream.

You can waft lower lower back to sleep and remember your preceding dream as in case you were having a dream.

For MILD, the maximum critical hassle is to don't forget your previous dream as in case you have been lucid. Many human beings speak approximately repeating the idea that you may have lucid desires again and again once more in advance than going to mattress. However, this is not the exceptional technique as it does not stimulate the thoughts in the identical manner because of the truth the MILD approach. It is viable to create a connection with the dream you clearly had and believe it as lucid. This will allow our mind to endure in thoughts that lucid goals are possible. We educate ourselves via asking "If you may lucid dream, what would it not have been like?".

It is easy to appearance how MILD works. After having a dream that become no longer lucid, the mind creates a highbrow photograph of itself having a lucid dream. This locations the thoughts in a revolutionary u . S . And lets in you to revel in the revel in. Imagine that you have had a lucid dream. This brings lucid dreaming nearer and lets in our thoughts to peer it as feasible. We can allow our mind to lucid dream by using developing the reminiscence-creativeness connection.

BACK TO BED

The Wake Back to Bed (WBTB) method for lucid dreaming is strong. It permits the dreamer to have enough relaxation at the same time as first of all asleep, after which leap right proper right into a lucid nightmare after returning to mattress.

Our our our bodies and minds have a rhythm, no matter whether or not we're massive aware or asleep. The wave-like pattern we revel in at some stage in sleep, called the circadian rhythm, affects the manufacturing of hormones and neurotransmitters. Our circadian rhythm, that may be a ninety-minute sleep cycle, governs our goals. This sleep cycle may be prolonged counting on the sort of sleep cycles we are in a role to complete each night time time. These sleep cycles may be prolonged over a longer time frame. The longer they'll be extended, the more time in the REM phase one can also have and the much more likely dreams is probably remembered.

The manufacturing of certain hormones and neurotransmitters is likewise a key element of the sleep cycle. Although we do not realize everything approximately dreams, or why they exist, we do apprehend a number of the chemical strategies that motive them to feasible.

Our mind may be extra open to the dreamlike opinions we've got whilst we permit our frame to go through a few cycles of midnight sleep. As we've got referred to, our ranges of recognition increase because the night progresses due to the producing of acetylcholine or the discharge of GABA. This permits expend our stores of serotonin and GABA, which lessen reminiscence and are at their most stages in a few unspecified time inside the destiny of sleep. After a few nights of sleep, the WBTB technique is activated. This lets in our mind to lessen the quantity of reminiscence-fogging chemical compounds. This permits us to remember our dreams, or maybe be extra privy to them. The Default Mode Network (or DMN, as it's miles commonly stated) is the default tool that the thoughts makes use of to feature normally at the equal time as conscious and alert. Any disruption of this tool can bring about cognitive adjustments. Patients with dementia can also experience a failure of the DMN.

We allow our sleep cycles and awakening to permit us to be lucid. This indicators our frame and mind to put together for the day. These greater techniques decorate attention and reminiscence formation. The WBTB approach is a clean approach of coping with the sleep cycle and ordinary chemical strategies.

THE WAKE BACK TO BED METHOD (WBTB)

Sleep among four and 5 hours.

Get up early and set an alarm. Stay aware for 30 to 60 minutes.

Make it your aim to stay a lucid day.

Back to your bed

The lucidity!

It is critical to get sufficient sleep earlier than starting WBTB. That's why I suggest getting at least 4 to 5 hours of sleep earlier than getting up. This will come up with a few more sleep cycles earlier than your alarm is going off.

What need to you do while the alarm sounds? This is an important a part of the approach. After waking up, you need to be certainly wide unsleeping earlier than going again to sleep. Do an interest and get away from bed. Be privy to the sector round you. Physical exercising may be a excellent option, as it releases adrenaline which lets in with awareness.

After about an hour of being extensive huge wide awake, and earlier than going once more to mattress, set a purpose to have a dream that is lucid. Focus on what is lucid after which bypass again to sleep. Although your thoughts can be more active than normal even as you visit mattress, you may discover it less complicated to doze off after a couple of minutes.

The Cycle Adjustment Technique (CAT) is a variation of WBTB, created with the beneficial useful resource of Daniel Love. The cause of this approach, it's far just like WBTB, is to adjust your frame's circadian rhythm cycle. Instead of putting an alarm to evoke at a specific time every night time time time, you sleep at one of a type instances each night time. This pointers the frame into getting more REM sleep.

WILDING

Chapter 7: My Story (Exploring Lucid Goals)

My names Stef, in case you didn't understand, and I'm the author of

I've been education the area to govern their desires for a extraordinary few years now and it's in reality been a pleasure.

I've determined hundreds, and I've taught masses. I've pushed the limits of lucid dreaming in plenty of tactics, and located what works and what doesn't.

In no way do I comprehend the whole thing approximately lucidity, due to the fact no person ever can. There is ALWAYS extra to analyze with lucid dreaming and no one can ever 'grasp it'. Just in the equal manner that you can't grasp paintings.

You can get suitable at it, and you can examine the basics, the advanced stuff and the way to create adorable creations but you could't 'grasp it'.

It's generally a journey, and also you'll generally be coming across components of it you in no way knew existed. BUT that being stated, I've spent pretty some time (numerous years now) learning about all of the strategies, techniques and procedures you can make this lucid dreaming revel in deeper, better, and more profound.

Why you need to lucid dream

There are MANY reasons you'll need to learn how to lucid dream, and I'm now not genuinely going to go into intensity proper right here because of the fact the opportunities are you already are privy to it's first-rate. You already understand approximately the benefits, but absolutely in case you don't, proper here are the principle blessings of lucid dreaming:

•Control your dreams

 and decide what to dream about so that you can experience like a superhero. You'll experience power surging thru your veins and you'll want to DO greater together together with your dreams and existence!

•Stop having nightmares

so you get restful, non violent sleep every night time and awaken feeling refreshed as if you've really spent a week in a high priced spa!

•Practice actual lifestyles abilties

within the dream together with martial arts so you can get earlier and beat your competition, or exercise new competencies and beautify at them

•Compose cute tune

, eat lovable dream food or discover alien worlds so that you awaken with tremendous reminiscences that enjoy very actual. And you could indulge in subjects without guilt

•Meet with prolonged misplaced own family participants or buddies so you can percent that one greater unique moment with them

•Literally do whatever you could agree with

so you can awaken with lovely self notion growing recollections

There are of course masses of various blessings as well. But you probable understand all of that, otherwise you wouldn't be reading this manual.. So the question now, is the manner to you lucid dream BETTER?

Set your self for lucid dreaming success

Before we get into the primary 'meat' of this ebook, we need to speak approximately the way to set yourself up for lucid dreaming success. What I suggest with the useful resource of manner of this is you want to get prepared to have lucid desires.

To begin with, simply ensure you've have been given a jogging dream magazine subsequent on your mattress, and you're writing your goals down.

It's easy to overlook approximately this, and while you apprehend a manner to lucid dream, to sincerely now not write any dreams down but this is wrong.

Even if you in reality remember a whole lot of your dreams, you have to keep a dream journal to see in which you went incorrect. You can write things like what supplements you used, how they worked, the way you felt the morning after and so forth.

Also, things like experiments and lucid dreaming goals want to be written inside the mag, otherwise you'll in no way be capable of appearance again and word what you in all likelihood did, in that you're going right and what you're doing incorrect. Make feel?

So before we flow into any similarly, make sure you're maintaining a dream magazine, and that it's subsequent on your mattress so that you can effortlessly get right of entry to it.

Basic weight-reduction plan and fitness setup for dreams

•I'll keep this brief as it's without a doubt the basics, however in order to optimise your thoughts for lucid desires you'll likely

want to be taking a multivitamin each morning, in addition to an Omega 3-6-nine tablet.

•This gives your thoughts the whole thing it wants to nicely feature and repair itself and so on.

Another issue you could look at is turning into Vegan or in particular plant based

(not critical, however I've determined it permits in a large manner with highbrow and bodily health).

•Wake up early: About five-6AM appears to be the exquisite time to rouse in the morning which though offers you sufficient sleep in case you get to bed on time, however furthermore lets you enjoy most of the day and I locate my thoughts works fine waking up within the period in-between. Of path, check for your self and look at what your body responds properly to!

•Drink lots of water: Every day you have to drink at least 7-eight glasses of filtered clean water

, as this is without a doubt basics for any health plan! Your thoughts and body will sense higher, accept as true with me.

The GOLDEN rule for lucid dreaming control

This is probably one of the maximum vital topics you can discover approximately lucid goals. In a phrase, what you EXPECT to expose up, will take region.

Now, you may have already heard that however it's constantly nicely well really worth having a reminder. What I suggest thru that is that a few aspect you observed or consider will happen, typically will due to the fact your subconscious mind wants to be proper.

In lucid dreams the principle dream international (the physics, and the mechanism of the way the entirety works) is controlled with the aid of your unconscious mind. You're satisfactory a hint bit of a miles huge picture, on the equal time as you're lucid.

This way it's which encompass you're strolling round a modern international which you don't have any clue approximately, although it's without a doubt YOUR mind that's developing and controlling all of it. It's a peculiar idea, I understand however live with me proper right here.

The blueprint that your subconscious thoughts creates and controls the lucid dream from is.. Drumroll please..

Your subconscious ideals and expectancies about the world round you.

This approach that some thing you TRULY consider deep down about the region, will typically show up in a lucid dream. Now, of direction there are exceptions because of the fact dreams are very weird and don't continuously look at the 'policies' but in fashionable, your beliefs manage the dream.

For instance, in case you've been living on this planet for greater than five years or so (even after three hundred and sixty five days sincerely) you recognize for a FACT that in case you throw some element up in the air, it comes down. (Gravity).

You comprehend this due to the fact you've visible it all of the time and your whole existence, no longer some thing considered one of a type has ever happened, surely so notion has sunk into your unconscious in order that even in a dream, you count on matters to fall even as you throw them up.

This is why maximum novices warfare to fly in lucid dreams, and why your lucid desires appear like they're sometimes controlling you alternatively the alternative way round.

Understand this concept and your lucid goals will in no way be the same, because of the reality you're spread out the key of control. If you TRULY convince yourself which you're the only on pinnacle of factors, and that something you want to arise, you EXPECT to reveal up, you'll do top notch topics.

Try it subsequent time you're lucid.

Become lucid and then go searching you and discover a car as an example. Now, besides that at the equal time as you snap your palms, the auto will shoot up into the air, without you even touching it.

Then snap your fingers. Nine instances out of 10, in case you certainly believed it, the auto will shoot up and also you'll probably begin feeling all excited and on foot throughout the dream shouting and so forth (and then probably wake yourself up) however that's suitable enough!

So before we flow on, definitely endure that during mind. Think about the golden rule in advance than seeking to lucid dream, and the way your expectation will make the dream end up actual. It will help you whilst you get stuck. There were lots of goals wherein I've been lucid, however been sort of caught and out of area manage..

But simply remembering that golden rule helped me get again into lucidity and over again on pinnacle of factors. I belief 'Wait a minute, what do I EXPECT to appear now?' and then it does seem. It's nearly like magic and it's a excellent manipulate approach for identifying what the dream does.

Chapter 8: Advanced Lucid Dreaming Adventures And Evaluations

Here we're going to speak approximately topics you can do to make the lucid dreaming revel in greater immoderate and interesting. This is stuff which you likely haven't tried but, however if there can be a few aspect right here you've already tried, just skip that factor.

You shouldn't surely be reading this detail if you could't already lucid dream, so if this changed into covered with different ebooks about lucid dreaming or if you've supplied this on it's very own, learn how to lucid dream in advance than analyzing this next section.

From now on we'll anticipate that you could come to be lucid, and these techniques or thoughts are speculated to be attempted on the equal time as you're lucid already.

Manifesting dream characters and hacking their minds

Dream characters are those human beings or one of a kind topics (they might be extraterrestrial beings!) within a dream that essentially upload to the dreaming revel in. They're in reality additionally a part of your unconscious mind.

They may be very useful and you may have a observe masses about your self thru interacting with dream characters. Remember, due to the truth they're a part of YOU, they could represent specific components of your brain and psyche.

You want to, as an example communicate to the part of your thoughts that represents a worry you've got, and ask it WHY you have that fear and so forth..

As the individual developing your lucid dream, your dream characters can be made mostly on your non-public liking. You can pick out to have interaction together with your dream characters, or not. Now on occasion, they may appear to behave or be created with out your purpose. Most of the time genuinely your dream characters are created routinely through your unconscious mind, so that you don't without a doubt have any input. But you could learn how to manage it!

Your dream characters will frequently act apparently in reality independant of you, the dreamer.

As you walk via a lucid dream, it looks as if they're separate human beings, and characteristic their very own loose will. They can decide what to do and it's which incorporates you're interacting with actual real people.

In many strategies, dream characters upload extra depth to your dream due to the truth they allow you a greater interactive lucid dreaming revel in.

In a few techniques, dream characters may be likened to online game characters. In video video video games, you due to the fact the player get to pick out the appearance of YOUR unique avatar that allows you to will let you navigate via the video game. Likewise, there are numbers of other characters within the video game as a manner to be interacting in conjunction with your formerly decided on online game character.

This analogy the use of video game characters is similar to dream characters. Just just like the video game person that interacts with other characters internal the game, you because the lucid dreamer additionally have the opportunity to engage with numerous dream characters as nicely.

So, why could you need to create dream characters? Well, dream characters serve loads of talents. They may be very useful!

You due to the fact the lucid dreamer can create the characters which might be maximum applicable to the context of your lucid dream. Some others sense that dream characters are a instance of our psyches and deep private ideals and reminiscences. Because of this, dream characters have a way of disclosing loads about the unconscious 'dreams and dreams' of the lucid dreamer.

Try it next time you're lucid, find out a dream man or woman (we'll speak approximately the manner to create them in a 2d) after which ask them what they constitute!

It's a way of 'hacking' their thoughts. Just via asking them questions like that, you get interior your very own head even more, and the answers you'll pay interest can be simply unexpected. The super way of doing this is sincerely to turn out to be lucid using anything technique you want, discover a dream person and then ask them 'what are you?'.

How to create dream characters without troubles

Here are a few techniques that you could have better achievement at growing dream characters:

It is important to be aware that in advance than you even begin developing dream characters, it's vital to have a enterprise corporation keep close of lucid dreaming. You must be capable of regularly take manipulate of your dreams earlier than you even start the method of trying to create dream characters internal a dream surroundings.

1: Shapeshifting

Shape-shifting is a totally exciting way to create the dream characters which you desire. Essentially you'll be using any item internal your dream state. Shape-shifting truly involves WILLING that specific inanimate object into the dream character which you choice.

This can also furthermore take some exercising, however when you've carried out shapeshifting an item right into a dream person you can discover that this method is one of the coolest methods to create dream characters in a lucid dreaming surroundings. Start via definitely looking at a random item like a car, after which inform your self 'as soon as I click on my fingers, the car turns into a dream man or woman'.

Trust me, if you believe it strongly enough it will take area, and in reality you don't even need an lousy lot belief to get it to occur. Usually I could make this manifest simply with the useful resource of imagining the alternate or visualising the auto changing into the dream individual. You might possibly want to workout this one a bit and it is able to no longer paintings first time.

I discover the extra strongly you may visualise the exchange, the faster it takes region. It's additionally beneficial to stabilise the lucid dream earlier than attempting this, because the shape transferring can usually have a tendency to shake the cloth of the dream a piece!

2: Using Dream Doors

Imagine beginning a door for your lucid dream and engaging in inside the dark depths of the door and in fact pulling out the dream person that you desire. Seems pretty a long way-fetched, huh? Well, actually it's no longer.

Dream doors or portals

are a first rate way door to create a dream individual, you surely should have the expectancy that your dream individual is inside the back of that door. It's all based totally at the strength of your expectancies and intentions.

Start by the use of manner of turning into lucid, after which discover a door or portal. A portal should literally in reality be a window without a doubt, or a hollow or some thing that you could ENTER. Imagine pulling a dream man or woman out.. Or agree with a dream person virtually taking walks out of the door or window.

Now stare cautiously on the portal or door. Tell your self 'in a 2nd, a dream individual will walk thru that door' after which just stare on the door. But don't stare as if you're SEEING if it's going to paintings.

Stare at it as you may while watching for a chum to show up. As in case you KNOW it's going to take vicinity and that they're really round the corner, and also you're in reality ready to look them come round the corner. Imagine the feeling you've got internal you whilst you've truely referred to as your buddy you're meeting up with, and they stated they could see you and they're simply down the road. That feeling at the identical time as you test out the distance looking forward to to look them quickly.

That's the sensation you want to have whilst searching the dream portal or door. If you can get that feeling, you'll make this paintings I promise.

3: Ask the lucid dream itself

If you want a specific kind of dream individual in a dream, why not honestly absolutely ask for it? Yes, you may ask your dream to provide you with the dream person of your desire.

Remember, with lucid dreaming you're the pleasant on pinnacle of things most of the time. Your lucid dreaming enjoy is absolutely as a lot as you for the maximum detail. The dreamscape feeds off of your dreams and dreams.

Therefore, it is viable in an effort to honestly ASK your dream to create the characters that you want and recognize that the characters will appear.

With this method, you due to the fact the lucid dreamer need to have a deep information and understanding that the dream responds to you in order for this approach to artwork.

Dream commands

also may be used to do nearly anything in a lucid dream.

I've managed to experience some awesome topics absolutely through asking the dream to reveal me the ones subjects. In fact the dream itself can genuinely wonder you, and in case you ask the dream to reveal you some aspect you're now not looking ahead to? Oh man..

That's a large surprise right there. The dream is of course created by way of using your unconscious mind, and maximum human beings have NO IDEA how powerful and complex that a part of your thoughts without a doubt is.

By asking the unconscious to marvel you, you're taken on a rollercoaster of experience. It's like tumbling down the rabbit hole! So the subsequent time you're in a lucid dream, attempt asking the dream to wonder you, or create a dream person for you and masses of others.

4: Create an Image with Your Mind's Eye

Finally, the usage of your mind's eye at the same time as in a lucid dreaming country it's actually a fantastic way to create dream characters with out hassle.

Whether you pick out to colour an photo of the dream character that allows you to introduce it to a dream environment or probably using a college approach of piecing together someone is more your style, the complete component is that the vision of your dream character starts offevolved offevolved with you.

You surely want to recognize mainly what you need your dream individual to look and be like so as that allows you to create that in your dream global truth.

Ultimately, growing dream characters isn't always as hard as it can seem. Once you have got a employer draw close of lucid dreaming and recognize the significance of expectation and aim within the lucid dreaming approach, you'll be for your way to growing dream characters pretty really.

Try this next time you're lucid: Create a dream man or woman based totally on YOU. Or simply find out a replica of your self inside the lucid dream and communicate to yourself. You'll be surprised at what number of complicated and profound answers he/she has!

Chapter 9: Some Extreme Topics To Dream About

Here are some crazy subjects you could try to lucid dream about. These topics are going to be extreme thru the way, so make certain you're prepared.

1: Go to a social occasion with insects

The animal and worm worlds are left on the whole undisturbed all of the time! They probable have social gatherings too! Now earlier than the guys in white coats come to take me away to the satisfied farm, I imply in desires. In goals, you may interact with thoughts, animals, bugs and some factor else.

Find a meeting of wasps, and sit down down in on their tea celebration! It is probably very similar to Alice in Wonderland and also you'll locate yourself curious approximately their recollections, jokes and mannerisms. When I tell human beings such things as this in my motion pix or via electronic mail it may be funny. People have probably in no way tried such things as this and it could be massively distinct from what they've attempted earlier than in desires.

It's a wonderful manner of experiencing new subjects. Also with the aid of attempting subjects which may be to date from what yo've USUALLY performed in goals before, you're developing. Your lucid dreaming abilties are becoming more potent and you're becoming extra of a lucid grasp.

2: Enter a portray

Paintings and drawings are whole worlds ready to be entered in lucid dreams. You can genuinely walk into them much like you'd stroll right into a door. For those of you who've seen or have a have a look at Narnia recollections, (the voyage of the Dawntreader)it's like when they input the painting of the boat and are transported to the scene, with the water flooding into the room and proper away pulling them into the scene.

Often you could enter the portray or picture in a lucid dream definitely through strolling as a good buy because it and urgent yourself towards it. Sometimes but, if you're not sincerely looking forward to as a manner to do that, you'll turn out to be genuinely half of caught within the wall and that can be annoying.

three: Become superman and start a fight

If you've visible Superman then you definitely definately'll recognize how superb it want to appearance to be invincible and capable of fly at supersonic speeds. Next lucid dream, make your self into the superhero and fly round, stopping anybody who wants to prevent you!

Superman or distinct superheros are notable a laugh to emerge as and play around with. I like flying or transferring gadgets with my mind the usage of telekinesis!

4: Lift a skyscraper with one hand

Another superhuman ability. Lifting in reality heavy topics with in truth one hand is a not unusual use of lucidity. To practice this, in waking existence you're going to workout the superpower by using PHYSICALLY putting your hand on heavy objects, and imagining what it would experience like if you had been able to increase them consequences.

Practice surely placing your hand on a vehicle (during the day) and questioning 'I can raise this effortlessly if I sincerely strive). This primes your unconscious thoughts and ideals which will do the equal in lucid goals. Tell yourself that the heavy devices are really weightless, and you'll be capable of convey them!

5: Build a metropolis along side your thoughts

Just like whilst you have got been a toddler an you finished with Lego to construct small cities (or now not, I do now not recognize) you can construct a city together with your thoughts in a dream. Rise above the distance thru using flying up, and then stretch out your hand. Imagine the city is building itself however you're on top of things of what gets constructed.

You can build entire towns in seconds, and you can rapid ahead time to look how the people in them exchange and behave over the years. See what different houses they gather and what occurs to their lives!

6: Grow a forest on the facet of your hands

You can create life in exactly the identical manner you'd damage it in lucid goals. One of the most amusing sports activities is to expand things like timber or forests collectively with your mind powers. Look on the floor within the the front of you and consider the strength and existence pressure coming for the ground, through your body, via your hand and into the region you're looking at.

Imagine the life force building a existence form like a tree, and then pace it up. You can increase an entire wooded area in seconds, and you may even circulate your hand the opportunity way to contrary the manner and spot the timber grow once more into the ground.

7: Visit the yr 19013894

Most people have ideas about what the future might be like based totally genuinely films and recollections, however how correct are they? The reality is the future possibly seems NOTHING like we're imagining it, and might be finished special to a few factor we understand these days.

Ask the dream to reveal you 2308420325 years into the future and also you'll be amazed at what you give you. I've finished this several times and it's particular on every occasion.

One time there has been actually not anything, genuinely blackness (I guess in that truth, we wiped ourselves out with bombs?). Other times, it's been a lovely array of lighting and power, just like a firework display. I guess that could be a truth wherein we've controlled to show ourselves into herbal electricity and don't want human our our bodies any greater. See what your mind comes up with!

8: Ask the dream to take you to the start of existence

What became the area like at the very start of existence? Was it a huge bang, or did we evolve? Was there a writer? All notable questions which we just in no manner surely recognise for high quality. We can theorise, and some theories can seem much more likely than others but we virtually don't apprehend for a hundred%. In your subsequent lucid dream ask your mind to take you to the start of existence.

When you strive these things, make sure you write them down in a dream mag. This will help you note what various matters felt like. You'll additionally want to write down down ANY dream symptoms and signs or subjects that took place in greater than 2 dreams. This might be critical in a while.

In reality I'd without a doubt suggest in reality trying each of this stuff in separate goals so that you can deliver your thoughts the satisfactory danger of getting a completely particular experience on every occasion. You don't need those to intrude with eachother.

Chapter 10: Dream Portals And Teleporting Into Excellent Worlds

A lucid portal is a few factor inside the dream that would transport you from one location to another. (Or one time to every different). It's some factor you can step through or into, like a replicate or a doorway..

They also may be in other types like a slide, tube, trapdoor, hollow inside the ground, misty air of mystery and lots of others. They can are available many bureaucracy, but the key is that they generally take you somewhere right away.

They can be observed everywhere, but normally your mind will place them into locations that usually have entrances or doors you may walk through.

This is in reality the suitable possibility to check your lucid portals, discover an extended street with many homes on either side, and start beginning all of the doors to peer what's the opportunity aspect.

You'll fast find out that it's now not definitely a person's house, it could be a few other international. This is due to the fact your thoughts creates subjects through doorways in dreams that don't usually 'combo' with the relaxation of the dream.

How to discover and enter a lucid portal

Here's how you may locate dream portals effects, and use them to journey through a dream worldwide. Remember that the KEY with dream portals is expectation and notion. If you in reality consider a portal will take you somewhere, it will!

1: Decide wherein you need to move

The first step to the use of dream portals is considering wherein it is you need to move. Try and provide you with a smooth photograph of the location on your thoughts, earlier than you even try and find out a portal. Think approximately whether or not or now not or no longer you've been there before, or what's going to be there whilst you arrive.

The more emotional you may get your response, the higher. If you can get simply scared and nervous, OR virtually excited and happy approximately the element, you'll get there much less complicated. Emotions and expectations are the two maximum vital subjects in lucid goals.

2: Find a herbal doorway or setting up

In desires, there are almost always topics that replicate waking existence. These matters may be resultseasily used as portals, due to the truth dream physics are NOT like real international physics.

You can also need to open a tiny door to a mobile smartphone sales region and discover each different planet on the other side of the door. Here are some examples of natural openings or doorways:

•Door or door frames

•Trapdoors inside the floor

•Shower curtains or drapes in homes

•Any window in any building

•You need to draw a trapdoor with chalk at the floor

3: Expect to tour via it

Look at the entrance you've placed or created, and inform yourself: 'I'm going to journey through this portal and arrive on the opportunity aspect in my region (some aspect region you need to visit). Notice that you don't HAVE to determine wherein to go to! You can clearly allow the dream marvel you!

four: Explore the vacation spot

When you input the place on the opportunity element, without a doubt discover it manifestly and don't panic! It might not be precisely what you predicted however it want to be pretty close! If you clearly permit the dream surprise you, then explore it! You may be everywhere!

Focus on what you WANT to be there

Sometimes clearly walking via you'll discover random topics, and this can be correct in case you're truely looking for to find out and discover the dream but if you've have been given particular lucid goals and you're seeking to get a few element accomplished in this lucid time, it's crucial to recognition as you enter the lucid portal.

Making the dreams greater stable

Lots of people find that they certainly awaken too fast from their Lucid reports and find out it very tough to get again to their preceding intellectual country.

This is going to help those people through prolonging their desires. When you find your self fading out of a Lucid Dream, spin round immediate.

Stand immediate and truly spin spherical. Not too speedy, however not too sluggish each. Just spin at the speed you may in real lifestyles and at the same time as doing so, 'will' your self to live in the dream. Tell your self that you'll live in the dream, and extra frequently than no longer you absolutely will.

Spinning round in a lucid dream

This works with the aid of forcing you to focus on some thing bodily. Many of the dream stabilisation techniques art work in this way and even simply specializing in some factor precise like searching at the element for your palms at the same time as in a dream can prolong it. It focuses your mind and relaxes you forcing you to live under for longer.

Doing things like losing to the ground in a dream in hopes to stabilise and interest you could produce other consequences however. It's been referred to that 'falling down' simply makes you wake up – or THINK you've woken up; you have got a fake awakening. We'll keep on with the spinning method for now. Here's the manner to do it:

Step 1: Focus yourself and Set your intentions

The first diploma with that is to set your intentions which is probably which you need to come to be a hint more targeted inside the dream and in the end prevent your self from waking up proper now.

You don't want to rouse the second one whilst you've grow to be Lucid so you can spin spherical to make it final longer. That's the reason proper proper here so make certain to surely cement this to your thoughts earlier than you certainly spin.

The cause you need to cement the cause to your thoughts first is that people frequently find out that inside the event that they truly spin without any purpose they turn out to be in a random vicinity; they've modified dream scenes and don't understand wherein they will be of what actually occurred.

It have to have the opportunity effect if you spin to try to relax and stabilise and then while you prevent spinning you're balanced on the pinnacle of a skyscrape looking down!

Step 2: Spin!

This is in which you without a doubt spin spherical, at the same time as looking on the ground. Try not to shut your eyes within the dream as this nearly continuously ends in waking up or to 'faux awakenings' which aren't first-rate. Spin spherical at a moderate tempo searching on the ground.

Step 3: Reality take a look at/live calm

Once you've stopped spinning you'll find out that you're greater targeted and the dream seems to have become clearer.

If now not, try some different stabilisation technique like looking at your arms or rubbing them together and so on, however it must be a super deal clearer now. You might possibly want to reality check in the intervening time or loosen up and select a mild walk within the dream.

Some reality tests you may attempt at this degree are:

- Pushing your finger via your palm

• Reading textual content to see if you can apprehend it

• Checking your watch to peer if the time changes

• Looking spherical to appearance if some thing appears extraordinary to you

Using nutritional dietary supplements to stabilise the dream

If you're a long time lucid dreamer, the possibilities are you're seeking out some element MORE. You understand you could do more with lucid dreaming, you absolutely don't recognise how.

Well, supplements is probably the solution. With supplements, you can take your lucid dreaming to another degree. They're really useful! We are lucky in recent times because of the fact there are DOZENS of lucid dreaming pills within the marketplace. I want there were this many once I first started out out out.

Here's a summary of the most common lucid dreaming tablets and the way they art work:

There are many splendid drugs and nutritional nutritional dietary supplements to be had, and all of them have an impact on desires in slightly precise strategies. We'll offer an reason behind a number of the primary ones, and the most commonplace. There are actually masses of them available, and it's very vital to apprehend as a whole lot as you can about them in advance than you operate them, if unsure, don't use it.

1: Calea Zacatechichi (The dream herb)

This is a small Mexican plant which even as the leaves are ingested produces effective dream effects. It growth the clarity of the dream, makes it experience 'extra actual' and makes the dream ultimate longer.

It's additionally understand as the Dream Herb, Leaf of god, Bitter Grass and masses of others. It's stated to taste disgusting at the equal time as below the affect of alcohol in a tea, and that after it's smoked, the smoke can be very dry and difficult.

It's been said that the brilliant manner to take Calea Zacatechichi for dreaming is to weigh down the leaves and smoke them through a water filtered bong, preferably with ice to relax the smoke, making it smoother to soak up.

2: Vitamin B6

This is a nutrients complement it's far stated as a manner to make your dreams more exquisite, and especially beautify dream remember. It's every now and then recognize because the 'dream pill' because it's very powerful at improving your dream recollect, and assisting you to bear in mind what you dream approximately.

three: Galantamine

Galantamine is probably one of the extra harsh dietary dietary supplements you may attempt. Still well really worth a pass however endure in thoughts it is able to be a bit difficult for your frame and those report feeling a chunk unwell every so often in this one.

four: LucidEsc with the resource of Vividream

Lucidesc

is An effective, herbal lucid complement designed to help you end up lucid on the identical time as you sleep. This is sincerely a top notch one for everyone because it's now not harsh on your frame and it clearly works thoroughly!

5: Melatonin

Melatonin has the energy to have an effect on lucid desires in a large way. This is more of a hormone however I felt it ready in right here. It's the hormone that makes you revel in tired at night time and can be used to have deeper and more notable desires on the identical time as taken on the right dosage.

6: Mugwort

Mugwort is in fact greater of a herb

however I'd find it irresistible to be in this internet web page. It may be used to make a 'dream pillow and different lucid aids. Very reasonably-priced, not as powerful as other dietary supplements however.

7: Choline bitartrate

Choline can offer you with better dream reminiscence

however it has exclusive benefits as nicely. It is extra of a reminiscence boosting complement that has robust links to lucid dreaming.

8: DreamLeaf (The crimson and blue drugs)

These incredibly designed tablets

are modelled on the colours from The Matrix. Containing lively and powerful lucid dreaming components, they're a high-quality preference for novice lucid dreamers!

Get those nutritional dietary supplements

The excellent area to get the ones supplements is a post I wrote evaluating they all and reviewing the first-rate lucid dreaming dietary dietary supplements. It's an extensive put up but there are easy links to each supplement stated right here and lots more.

There are ALSO loads of discounts I've managed to get you guys so if you need to analyze greater about the ones dietary dietary supplements and get reductions, test out the 'e-book bonus' phase at the stop of this e-book, which has a completely unique list of reductions and information for you.

Stopping/slowing down time in desires

Do you need in order to manipulate your notion of time in a lucid dream? Turns out you may truely save you time on the identical time as you're lucid, and extend the lucid dream.

Time, in truth, is to three diploma, subjective. What might also look like a long time to as a minimum one person can appear like a brief time for every other. It relies upon at the men and women notion of methods slowly or rapid time is passing, and consequently in a dream, we want to be able to exchange our notion and therefore prevent time in a dream!

So to try this, as with most of the lucid guidelines validated in this internet internet page, you could of course need to be strong collectively with your fact exams, and the equal old topics you will do to turn out to be lucid and live alert inside the dream. I don't want to remind you approximately all of that stuff.

Chapter 11: Shout Out 'Stop Time!' To The Dream Itself

Believe it or now not, while you are lucid,

shouting out commands

like 'save you time' truly artwork masses of the time. Because you're almost speaking in your unconscious thoughts you are capable of be quite specific about what you want to take vicinity.

By in reality shouting out to the dream global, you may get maximum of your instructions replied, however there are a whole lot of times in which this will not work. If you are now not lucid enough and also you do no longer do not forget a few factor will alternate, it may not, It's lots like in The Matrix in which Neo is studying to 'make the leap'.

Any small doubts approximately his capability and he's going to fall, and it's far this that applies proper right here. If you shout out a command like 'time will prevent' to the dream, and you're simply type of ready to look if it'll take region, it probable won't. You need to shout it out as in case you're first rate it will seem.

Almost like you recognize beyond a doubt that point will stop. If that is proving tough, then you definately in reality may moreover need to try a few considered one of a kind thoughts earlier than you may definitely make time come to an entire halt. Dreams are a elaborate element to grasp, but it's far all possible.

You'll additionally discover that the more you analyze and the maximum you try to range the capabilities you research, the faster you could improvement.

Slowing down time in a dream

So in case you're suffering with preventing time clearly, you could discover it less complex to simply sluggish it down before the whole lot. Slowing it down will make it appear like anyone else round you is transferring slower glaringly, however you'll be shifting at ordinary pace.

There's commonly a hint little bit of confusion with slowing down time or preventing time, because of the truth considered certainly one of matters are happening to you. (This has been established in movies which includes X-Men, Days of destiny past).

•You make time come to a halt, however you can float around at normal pace

OR

•You speed YOURSELF as much as such an quantity that the whole thing else seems to be frozen but in reality you're surely transferring in reality, truly fast

In the dream, it doesn't in fact rely which of these two take area, because of the truth with each of them, you will subjectively enjoy time slowing down or stopping. This brings me to the technique you will be using the slow down time in a dream.

It's all about your emotions and your thoughts. You're going to 'expect' clearly speedy'. Instead of specializing within the vicinity round you and on the lookout for to make that each one gradual down, you may pace your self up and this will in turn gradual the rest of the arena down.

Some affirmations or thoughts you'll need to begin having at this degree are:

•'I'm transferring so speedy that everything round me is on occasion moving in any respect'

•'I can pass at lightning velocity throughout the dream global'

Saying the ones each to your head to yourself or out loud within the dream will start slowing time in the dream. While pronouncing or wondering these statements, strive jogging or transferring round as well, search around you for strategies to test how speedy you're going.

Maybe discover a dream man or woman, run round him and tap him at the decrease lower returned, then zoom spherical to the the the front earlier than he can turn.

At this thing, he should be transferring actually slowly. (Or you are shifting very quickly) and it'll deliver the enjoy of time having slowed down.

Your belief of time is based absolutely around the assets you do and the places you move in a dream, so as you are capable of excursion rapid - Almost without delay - Time can appear to be it is going by manner of way of quicker and you're spending longer inside the dream.

Interesting lucid dreaming experiments

When you get into superior lucid dreaming, one of the BEST subjects you can do is to set your self desires and traumatic situations to do. It's all thoroughly just flying spherical, however you may want to push your self to do extra in the long run.

What you could do, is to set yourself those goals before you visit bed and then try to acquire them to your lucid goals. Here are a few very exciting desires or experiments you may strive in a lucid dream:

1: Telling your dream characters they're in a dream

What do you consider you studied ought to seem at the same time as you tell your dream man or woman they're in a Lucid Dream?

Would they emerge as Lucid with you?

Well, it surely is predicated upon on how conscious and on top of factors you are, but in case you're on top of things and you've grounded yourself nicely in the dream the dream characters can also end up Lucid with you.

It's a manner of advancing via the awesome 'layers of a lucid dream' and going deeper into your thoughts. I'm no longer going to inform you what truly takes location with this one as I count on it's more interesting to strive it with out searching beforehand to three issue precise to take place.

I'll warn you presently even though, it's going to be excessive and you'll WANT to make sure you're capable of write your desires down within the morning. This isn't always a dream you'll want to neglect. Having stated that I don't suppose you'll be ABLE to miss this one very with out issues.

2: Talking to your nightmares

Ever been so afraid of a few thing which you in reality can't stand even thinking about it, not to say talking about it? For me, it become dogs, and wasps.

I became afraid of them, however then in a Lucid Dream, I decided a dog and literally requested it, 'Why am I scared of you' and it answered a few problem along the traces of 'you have been chased through one as a young toddler and you haven't sincerely consistent the concern that got here due to that. You additionally have minor receive as proper with issues, so you don't recall that puppies won't chase once you once more'.

Pretty eye commencing for me, and the equal form of aspect happened when I requested a wasp the identical detail in a dream. Turns out I have been given stung after I changed into 4 and will have died.

I attempted to select out up a wasp, because of the reality I idea it seemed quite and favored to pup it, it then stung me and (because the wasp explained inside the dream). I therefore developed slight recollect troubles and a deep seated fear of wasps. It took YEARS for me to restore that hassle and Lucid Dreaming is straight away chargeable for helping me with that.

I find that sort of factor charming. The reality that you can at once engage with or maybe CHANGE fears and phobias simply thru speaking to them without delay in a dream. It opens up the door to all types of different questions, and also you start questioning simply how a incredible deal you can exchange about your mind with lucid goals.

3: Look into a replicate!

When you take a look at a replicate in real lifestyles, you be conscious that it's an specific example of you, (manifestly). The laws physics are at play and so you MUST see exactly how you appearance.

In a dream of route physics and some other criminal guidelines are non-existent, consequently searching into a reflect in a dream can display you loads approximately yourself and the way you're feeling about yourself.

It's

 a chunk bit like your residual self image

, which I've spoken approximately earlier than. A blueprint of what you placed you need to seem like stored in your thoughts. Finding a reflect permits you to look in awesome detail exactly the kind of man or woman you observed you are.

The horrifying component but, is that every now and then we're able to see matters which we commonly forget about about about in a dream reflect. We can considerably exaggerate physical flaws and imperfections and it could appearance in reality frightening.

4: Speak to a psychiatrist/counsellor

Your unconscious mind is a charming difficulty to speak to. Really, clearly are in search of a city for a counsellor in a dream and take a seat down and speak to them. It will display subjects to you which you by no means ought to have realised in advance than.

You can also form of ask the dream questions, and it usually will respond with some aspect exciting. You don't actually need to recognise particularly the manner to discover a dream manual or counsellor, due to the fact your thoughts will work it out. Just walk round saying out loud 'in which's my dream counsellor' and you'll discover it.

five: Travel in time and meet your self in the future

This is a in reality top notch test to find out what you absolutely consider your dreams and aspirations.

Do you TRULY be given as genuine with you'll acquire your goals and desires? If so, you'll meet a sophisticated, a success and exceptional model of yourself within the destiny and you'll awaken feeling inspired and inspired.

If you don't be given as proper with in your self, it'll come out in the dream. You can't trick your unconscious mind, (without problems) and often it is going to show you a merciless instance of your beliefs and mind towards your self.

Convincing a dream person they're in a dream

What takes area on the same time as you convince a dream person that they're in a lucid dream?

Convince them that their international isn't actual...

You ought to pretty without problems display it to them, so what could they do after they realise it? Telling a dream character that they're no longer actual and it's all a dream is an great test to attempt in your next lucid dream.. Here's what happened as soon as I tried it:

Chapter 12: Convincing A Dream Individual To Come To Be Lucid With Me

This is the story of a dream I these days had once I convinced a person his worldwide wasn't actual. I began the dream off like some other, with the useful resource of manner of doing a fact take a look at at the same time as within the center of some random motion, I suppose it changed into sitting at a desk with my friend and as were have been discussing the weather I checked out my fingers.

This added on a reality take a look at, I even have come to be without delay aware that this wasn't real, and so I appeared up at my buddy, and requested him 'Where did we clearly come from?'.

•'What do you propose? We definitely got here from metropolis.. We spent the day buying, don't forget?'

•No, we didn't. I concept approximately the way to provide an reason behind this to him..

•'We're in a dream' – 'This isn't actual'.

He regarded stressed, nearly a touch scared, now not scared that it's a dream, but scared that I'm crazy or appearing weird. Just to make certain of myself, I did every one-of-a-kind fact test, and my finger surpassed via my palm.

'This actually is a dream, and I can show it', I said this now not pretty statistics what to expect.

As I used telekinesis to move a plate throughout the desk, he subsequently agreed that this was in truth a dream. This is whilst it were given bizarre for me.

He snapped into a very specific man or woman. As if his body had simply been possessed, and checked out me at once in my eyes. 'What are you doing in right here.. In this part of your mind?'. He shouted this at me.

I didn't understand what to mention.

Who modified into this dream character now representing?

What part of my thoughts have grow to be he?

I had no idea, and started out out to assume I have become a touch out of my depth, however I stored on. I defined that I recognize it's a dream and preferred to appearance what should arise if I knowledgeable him. We then went for a stroll outdoor, and what come to be the door changed into an extended hall.

This stretched on for what regarded like miles, and as we walked I persevered to ask him what he represented.. He wouldn't tell me, but insisted that I changed into 'On the right direction'. Although I turn out to be conscious and genuinely in control, after I attempted converting subjects he stopped me..

I attempted shifting scenes and just teleporting away, however he had a few form of effective power that held me in region.

I turned into no longer capable of shipping.

It clearly got a piece scary, and at one point I tried to awaken, however I couldn't. It have become like being trapped inner my very own thoughts.. I knew thoroughly that my frame have become laying there, asleep, and yet even though I become lucid I couldn't ruin faraway from this dream person who had grow to be powerful and aware.

He confident me that it's suitable enough, and there's not anything to worry approximately, so we saved on foot. Through each of the doorways, he confirmed me some issue I had discovered out from the past. A lesson determined from numerous conditions or sports, and he said that it modified into 'the start of a completely precise journey'. 'Lucid Dreaming is simplest the start' he said.

As we walked, we persevered to talk, and he gave me a few advice and powerful insights into my thoughts and the manner it worked which I can't share proper here as it's some distance too non-public, however what I can say is that

i

t's as despite the fact that your thoughts is ready unfastened. I don't realise what's happening scientifically proper right here, however all I realise is that I modified into lucid inner my thoughts, and I had satisfied each unique a part of my mind that 'it' too want to end up lucid.

The gateway to 'The large photograph'

This is probably the most profound problem I've finished in lucid dreaming up to now. It's nearly existence changing, however I won't carry on lest you think I'm exaggerating or making it up.

Try it for yourself, make sure you're truly aware and stable within the dream yourself, and then persuade a person they're in a dream.

See what part of your thoughts it will become and what's going to expose up. Remember, despite the truth that at times it could seem horrifying, or maybe a piece bit unstable at the same time as you assume you 'can't escape the dream', you may by no means get caught in a lucid dream, don't worry about that. Just lighten up, and experience the trip.

It's opened my mind in a manner that's in no way occurred before, all due to the fact I informed a dream individual he's in a dream. I strongly recommend that everybody who's even a piece bit into lucid dreaming ought to do that, because it's special for every person.

Dissolving the dream country (INTENSE)

I've been controlling my goals for some years now however this changed into some problem truely new to me. I controlled to 'move past' the dream kingdom and in reality dissolve the dream nation into natural hobby.

This is more of a hint story than an educational, because of the fact that is something that you could sort of guess a way to do your self whilst you're lucid. It's self explanatory, except proper proper here's the tale:

Before I begin explaining this great dream I had, I need to make it smooth that that is actually my revel in and my description of what I professional.

I'm now not making specific claims that I've achieved enlightenment, reached 'natural focus' or whatever like that. I'm genuinely going to give an reason behind the dream that I had, make of it what you'll.

It started out out as a regular dream..

It started out out out as I was having a normal dream. I were given into bed and begin to loosen up. I wasn't looking for to spark off lucidity, I become genuinely really worn-out and preferred to sleep. Some nights are like that, you don't need to TRY and lucid dream, you in reality type of 'permit pass' to the bed and just go together with the flow into dream international.

I laid there for approximately 5 mins and then commenced to lose recognition. I wasn't looking for to live aware, so this wasn't a hassle.

A few hours later

(I'm guessing, due to the reality I awakened quickly after the whole dream at about 9AM)

I began to have a chain of extended, complex goals.

These dreams have been slightly personal, so I won't proportion all the records, however they have been a combination of reliving artwork days, some conversations with numerous ex-companions and an adventure to try and energy over a few water.

Random stuff, I comprehend. After the ones desires, I find out myself strolling down a street in a crowded city. I seize the pondered picture of myself in one of the domestic domestic home windows and phrase that a few element is a chunk atypical about my blouse.

It's a small element, but it makes me think about how I got to in which I come to be. 'How did I get to this street? I don't recall on foot here' I asked myself.

So then I did a reality test. I attempted to push my finger thru my palm, (that is my most effective reality check) and without delay have emerge as lucid.

Now, at this element, I ought to mention that it wasn't just a ordinary lucid dream. The 2nd I actually have come to be Lucid, I knew something became precise. It felt sharper, greater vibrant and really actual. It felt nearly like I couldn't wake up even though I desired to.

In most lucid dreams, all of the at the same time as you're lucid you've got were given an less expensive draw close to at the state of affairs and if you need to awaken, you typically can. That have emerge as no longer the case in this dream. I seemed spherical and started manipulating matters. The maximum fun detail for me currently in lucid desires is to move gadgets with my thoughts the usage of telekinesis.

I started out out lifting small gadgets and transferring them spherical. I had no 'goal' at this factor, I have come to be simply taking part in being lucid and loose. I became taking part in in reality being in my very very own little international and playing spherical. Some desires are like that, you really want to be playful and experience your self.

So the dream went on, and I persisted exploring. The longer I stayed inside the dream, the clearer it have emerge as. I started out to get used to the feeling of it and it felt like I'd been there for hours, possibly even days. As I explored an increasing number of I fell in love with the sensation.

It turn out to be precise to my one of a kind lucid dreams. This one truly felt 'right'. I felt like I changed into precisely in which I needed to be at that point, regardless of the fact that I didn't complete understand what became taking location.

Manifesting cash and controlling dream characters

I tried diverse subjects out from this element on. Firstly, I were searching for to make extra money at paintings the past few weeks, so this went via to my dreaming mind.

I started out out manifesting coins in my hand. I imagined a stack of £50 notes and that they regarded in my hand. I threw them away and started out out to increase wood from the ground.

I'd observe wherein I desired to expand the tree, keep my hand out and push a load of energy through the air into the floor. The tree at once started to extend and inner some seconds it changed into towering above me. Pretty cool, however I wanted to do more.

I mess around some greater and start to manipulate the possibility dream characters. I decide in which they're going to walk and what they're going to mention. This is fun for some time. After a few minutes of this, I maintain my fingers out to my elements and look up at the sky. I enjoy so effective, and however so loose at the equal time.

It's all very smooth. I marvel at this thing how I've now not woken up but, as I've performed pretty some thrilling topics and generally I can tell once I'm about to evoke fro the lucid state. Not this time. This time the dream sincerely stayed placed. I couldn't shake it if I preferred to.

I appeared decrease lower back at the sky and started to drift lightly on my lower returned. At this stage I felt in reality relaxed. I felt like a king searching down on his united states of america of the us from his fort.

Trying to find out my dream manual

When I came another time to a status position, I actually have become someplace new. I had some humans strolling through me and I decided to try to discover my dream manual.

The SECOND I had this perception, the scene seemed to proper away alternate. I placed the dream characters take a look at my otherwise, as although they had woken up or they knew some thing I didn't.

I search around and some human beings look over again at me. I don't say a few aspect, but I actually have the aim of locating my dream guide. Someone to assist me through the dream and supply me some mind as to what to do subsequent. After all, this seemed like a sturdy dream and I didn't need to waste it any more with the useful resource of the use of throwing automobiles round.

After some seconds, a bizarre man seems to in reality appear at my side and appears at me as even though he's checking that I'm alive. It's like he's searching for to schooling consultation if I'm clearly right here or no longer, and it's very off-setting and unusual for me.

Chapter 13: A Conversation With My Lucid Dream Manual

I ask him if he's a dream manual and he says 'Yes of route I am'. He takes me to a futuristic searching metropolis and we stroll to a area wherein there's a form of vital 'square' or clearing. Skyscrapers upward push up into the clouds all round us and the metropolis is alive with noises and masses of motion.

We then have a communication as people (aliens, robots and businessmen) stroll round us going about their day..

Me – Where are we?

Dream Guide – 'This is the 'front'. This is in which human beings enter the dream and connect to do commercial enterprise enterprise offers of every type'

Me – What do you mean? What kind of commercial business enterprise offers?

Dream Guide – (I can't don't forget the proper way he said this however I'll attempt) 'Well, humans from all around the universe come together right right here amongst other places, to do commercial business corporation gives. Some of them have transcended time and that they get collectively proper right right here to artwork on 'timelines' and 'recuperation matters' in information'

Me – 'Wow, that's incredible. Why did you deliver me right proper here?'

Dream Guide – (Again at this factor he seems into my eyes and looks to be 'checking' that I'm in fact fame there and no longer actually an illusion) 'I anticipate you're prepared to look this. I've been searching you increase, over again in your lucid dreams, and I expect you're prepared for the following step'

Me – What do you mean, 'again in my dreams'?

Dream Guide – 'If you haven't located, you're no longer the simplest dreamer on this area'

Me – 'What are you talking about, that is my dream! I'm on top of things here I'm simply letting you show me some thing'

Dream Guide (At this element he appears at me the way a figure must have a look at a infant mastering to stroll, a type of loving, statistics look) – 'We have been on your dream, however I've brought you here to analyze some thing'

At this diploma, multiple one in all a kind people enter our communication. We're truly reputation there inside the center of this place on this futuristic city, and a person wearing a wholesome with every different guy sporting a leather-primarily based-based totally trench coat arise to us.

They inform me that they're dreamers too, and that I should be cautious with pointing out that it's my dream and I'm on pinnacle of things in this area. It might be volatile, they tell me. Now, I haven't organized for a deep dream like this.

The previous night time I have been ingesting a bit bit, and I hadn't completed any form of meditation or prep paintings for this, so my dreaming thoughts is a piece off key. I'm now not really thinking about what I'm doing, so to talk.

I begin to speak decrease again and argue that it's certainly my dream, and I'm on top of factors. With one flick of his hand he lifts me about 6 ft up into the air.

He's the usage of telekinesis on me! That's my element!

I hang there within the sky, powerless.

I can't bypass in any respect, and I am nevertheless absolutely lucid.

I'm not dropping popularity and I'm nevertheless very hundreds privy to what's taking place, and (I concept) on top of things. He places me down gently and goes right away to explain that it's now not absolutely all and sundry's dream, however that we're all here collectively in this region.

I'm amazed.

I don't understand what to mention, and so when I get located down on the ground I go taking walks. I walk out of the city and into a barren location vicinity. I don't have a purpose for wherein I'm going at this factor I definitely want to get lower lower back to somewhere 'everyday' some factor this means that.

Dissolving the dream state

At this stage within the dream I'm blown away. I don't recognise what's happening any greater and I do some truth exams to make truly exquisite that I'm dreaming, and I am of course. I can nevertheless fly, I can though expand bushes and create money however for some motive again there inside the town I become overpowered.

It's no longer like I modified into looking for it both, I modified into completely on top of factors of my emotions, thoughts and ideals and but I simply couldn't do some thing.

Strange. That's in no manner came about in advance than, however it have become about to get higher..

I'm within the barren region clearing and I search around me. I experience humbled, sort of like I've definitely come out of a deep meditation consultation and I'm feeling 'in love' with the region. I feel amazing! But it's extra than exquisite, and from this factor on some thing that I've never professional in advance than began to take location.

I started out out to experience EVERYTHING. All right away. But 10 times higher, larger and greater effective

When I say 'everything', I recommend it like this:

•Imagine for a 2d the closing time you laughed

 till you cried, and you felt intensely happy or cherished

•Now agree with the remaining time you orgasmed

 or had intercourse

•Now the final time you have been heartbroken

 or out of place a friend/family member/pup, some factor

•Now accept as true with the final time you felt surely happy or loved

 .. The feeling of water inside the direction of your frame at the equal time as you swim inside the sea, the sensation of ice bloodless water as you drink on a warm summers day, and the entirety in amongst.

Now bear in mind ALL of those topics, all of the ones moments of emotional fee, ALL AT ONCE, except x100.

Imagine feeling the intense pride, the pain, and it's all combined together and amplified through approximately 10 times. It's overpowering and I can't perform a little thing with it, apart from just allow it arise and sincerely deliver in to this enjoy.

I fall lower lower back, powerless and overwhelmed and lightly waft above the floor, searching up on the sky. The sky isn't always a mixture of blue location and clouds but is actually a white glowing mild.

Everywhere I appearance is white. It's actually white power, all spherical me. It's now not the same form of white mild which you'd expect, it's extra like being underwater and SURROUNDED through way of the slight. You can't examine it or cognizance on it as it IS your popularity.

It's the entirety you're aware of and you could't popularity on everybody a part of it, because it's best ONE detail.

I don't even try to recognition on it and as a substitute attention at the emotions surging through me. Those immoderate feelings are in spite of the reality that speeding thru me at a constant fee. They don't slow down, they virtually live there constantly. It doesn't damage as such, it surely feels splendid. Like I've been given a big, powerful power and it's overcoming my complete frame.

I'm unexpectedly privy to everything. I experience my body slumbering in bed, I enjoy the limitless opportunities of dream adventures round me. I see great white strength however I'm aware of lots more than that. I can without a doubt experience everything, and I can see my entire lifestyles's reminiscences laid out inside the the the front of me.

It's like they're truly all being verified to me at the same time, type of like if you have been in a room with one hundred TV video display units all gambling unique films on the same time. Normally that could be no longer possible to cognizance on, but on this dream I can also additionally want to apprehend and focus on they all at the identical time.

I feel my growth as someone, I see my maximum lovable memories. Some that I didn't even recognize I had. I experience like I'm crying, but it's now not in reality crying due to the opportunity emotions and power surging via me. Whatever this united states of america turn out to be, it felt genuinely incredible and I never wanted it to end.

It's like I'd transcended the entirety I knew to be real, and I was loose. This end up the primary time I'd dissolved the dream country like this, and I am now going to attempt it every time I lucid dream. I looking for recommendation from this dream as 'lucid transcendence'.

Notes approximately the dream:

The night time earlier than I'd had a few drinks with a pal, so it may had been a 'REM rebound' lucid dream. I started the dream generally and have end up lucid through doing the 'finger via the palm' reality check. As the dream stepped forward I constructed on the stability via using grounding myself and respiratory deeply.

So it turn out to be pretty excessive but searching over again, that emerge as the begin of my barely extra excessive lucid desires. From then on I've been having masses greater of those types of goals, pretty often.

They now not fine make me wake up feeling passionate about lifestyles and energised, however they open my eyes as to the possibilities of this worldwide and the concept that there may be plenty extra accessible that we really can't enjoy or first-class as human beings.